C000242863

Casting A Queer Circle

Casting A Queer Circle

Circle

Non-Binary Witchcraft

Thista Minai

Hubbardston, Massachusetts

Asphodel Press
12 Simond Hill Road
Hubbardston, MA 01452

Casting A Queer Circle: Non-Binary Witchcraft
© 2017 Thista Minai
ISBN 978-1-938197-21-5

All rights reserved. Unless otherwise specified,
no part of this book may be reproduced in any form
or by any means without the permission of the author.

Distributed in cooperation with
Lulu Enterprises, Inc.
860 Aviation Parkway, Suite 300
Morrisville, NC 27560

Be only what you are,
and be all that you are.

Contents

Foreword

The world of is teeming with energy, magic, passion, and purpose. Our veins pulse with iron in our blood core that mirrors the iron rolling in the center of the earth, and we shed salted tears like the waves that splash against the shore. As our lungs fill up we are tuned into the possibilities of cool breezes and cyclones alike, and our passion and temperature fluctuations alike can mirror warm coals and raging bonfires.

Magical practices and traditions do not always create safe and encouraging spaces for everyone to tie into energy, magic, passion, and purpose; to connect with their spirit, or feed their faith. Whether they fall outside of a gender binary experience or a heterosexual framework, various Pagan traditions create an unconscious (or occasionally conscious) hostility.

When the God demands to be seen as the erect phallus, and the Goddess nothing but a vast womb, men who were assigned female at birth and women who were told they were boys are excluded. When all magic is said to be charged with a polarity rooted in that God and Goddess being lovers, where is the space for the power of resonance, for women who love women and men who love men?

In *Casting a Queer Circle*, Thista Minai is tackling some of these questions, but do not be fooled—this book is not just for those who are coming from a variety of LGBTQAI+ populations. These concepts merely inform the beginning of a dive down into new approaches and ways to engage with magic on a different level. The tools presented in this book create new systems for building covens, techniques for casting circles, and open up doors to magic that deserve to be seen by the world.

Over my twenty-five years in public Neopagan communities, I have seen a wide variety of approaches to magic and ritual. Many of them, however, are rooted in an unconscious bias against the diversity of the human expression. By unlocking opportunities for further diversity of magical expression, this book takes on some of the challenge that Yvonne Aburrow argues for her *Inclusive Wicca Manifesto*: "Inclusive Wicca is not for people who want to stay safe and cozy in their heteronormative cisgender worldview, pretending that oppression is not happening and that racism is a thing of the past."

By moving towards a form of inclusive Wicca, this project pushes us each towards being more inclusive in our world at large. It is not just in our worship of the God(esse)s that we have an opportunity to shift the world, but it can be in Their honor that we shift the world. The systems Thista and the Spectrum Gate Mysteries coven uncovered and have exposed for use here can help us each, as Thista says, "take what works, and shape it into something that helps you get what you need." This is in and of itself a core expression of freedom, and is also a call to Feminist witchcraft, wherein all people can and should engage in magic and will-work from a way that is true to their core and power.

It is time for the world to move beyond the notion that the chalice and the blade are the only path to fertile connection and creation. The world deserves more flavors than one, even if that flavor is one that many folks can and should still use if it calls to them. It is time for each of us to craft our own queer circles, with queer not just entailing an orientation or a gender experience in this case, but a step beyond the expected – for what is magic after all but a harnessing of our own will using intention, attention, and aligned actions or ritual?

Make this calling to magic yours. Truly yours. This is not cookie-cut magic, but an invitation to inclusion of your own spirit. Open up your eyes, and step forward. You too can cast your own queer circle, no matter your journey.

Yours in Passion And Soul,

LEE HARRINGTON
MAY 2017

Author of Traversing Gender: Understanding Transgender Realities; Sacred Kink: The Eightfold Paths of BDSM and Beyond; *and co-editor of* Queer Magic: Power Beyond Binaries.

Coven Craft Basics

Our Story

Today there are many traditions of magic, witchcraft, and ritual that operate in covens or other small groups. A person who wants to find a system to practice has many choices, and many of them welcome people of any sex, gender, identity, or orientation. Yet some individuals are yearning for a path that helps them dive in deeper, or in a different way. Due to this yearning, the Spectrum Gate Mysteries were built.

With so many paths out there, why did our coven feel the need to create our own system rather than learning one that is already available? Crafting a complete and coherent ritual system is a *lot* of work, so why bother? Part of the problem may have been access and accessibility. Queer-friendly ritual systems that embrace wide varieties of personal expression exist, and if you are part of one, fantastic! Diversity is a strength. The more different types of ritual that exist out there for seekers to choose from, the better.

But when I began my spiritual education, I didn't know of any queer-friendly traditions, and didn't yet recognize the queerness in myself. My upline—the ritual system I was trained in—is traditional Wicca. Throughout the vast majority of my training, I understood myself only as a cisgender woman, and as such, was able to find reasonable comfort in Wicca's inherently binary system. However, along that journey were many points at which I questioned my gender, feeling there was something that didn't quite fit right. Each time I posed that question, I would wander farther away from what it meant to be a woman in our society, but even finding myself identifying as a gender nonconforming woman, I could still function as a Wiccan Priestess, so all was well.

Shortly after I received my third degree rank in Wicca, that fell apart. I stumbled into a community of queer, trans*, and otherwise non-binary folk who opened my eyes to an entirely new way of experiencing and expressing identity. I began to understand sex, gender, orientation, and presentation as four different things, sometimes related or interconnected, but different nonetheless. As I examined these concepts within myself, I swiftly understood what hadn't felt quite right before: my sex is female, but my gender is not, and my presentation struggled to express that. I dis-

covered that my gender is neither woman nor man, but something else
entirely.

Suddenly, Wiccan ritual didn't always suit me anymore. It didn't en-
compass the totality of who I am. As long as I wanted to focus on my
physical body, I could still be a priestess, but what about when I wanted to
focus on my identity instead? I briefly considered going through all of the
elevations in Wicca once more as the other gender, thinking this might
help me achieve a more neutral state as an initiate, but I quickly realized
that initiating as a man would not solve my problem of wanting to be present in circle as a "something else". I knew that there were other
genderqueer folk in my tradition who had adapted in ways they found ful-
filling, so I started to ask what they did and how it worked.

What I learned was that they picked whether they wanted to be priest
or priestess depending on how they felt, and that was enough for them. It
was not enough for me. In my mind, the roles of priest and priestess are
inherently gendered, if for no other reason than that "priest" and "priestess"
are gendered words. In both magic and society, words have tremendous
power, so I was not content to consider it semantics and nothing more. I
needed a better solution—a ritual system that would allow me to stand in
ritual as an officiator that was neither man nor woman. I needed to feel
that my gender was just as important as any other gender, and to feel represented and celebrated in ways that systems with binary language could
not provide.

Around this same time, I began working with the two people who
would become the other core members of the Coven of the Spectrum Gate.
One of these identifies as genderqueer, and the other is intersexed. Both
understood and shared my discomfort with the terms "priest" and "priestess". We wanted new officiating roles that did not carry historical baggage
attached to concepts of binary gender, and in doing so we hoped that we
would find ways to engage with magic and ritual outside of a required binary in general.

To be clear, we do not feel that the terms "priest" and "priestess" need
to be abandoned entirely. Plenty of men and women find the terms "priest"
and "priestess" powerful and useful, and I have no desire to take that away
from them. For myself, my female sex is still an important part of my

overall identity, and I still often refer to myself as a priestess. Our intent was not to change the available options, only to increase them.

We began by searching for other words for a ritual officiator that didn't carry connotations of gender, but we weren't able to find any that we liked. In looking more closely at what a priest and priestess actually did in the casting of a circle, we also started to think about how we might want to rename those roles. What we discovered was that we wanted new roles altogether. The more we looked critically at how Wiccan circles are cast, the more we felt that we wanted to go about the division of labor in a fundamentally different way. We wanted roles based on and named for the function they performed, and we determined that the function of our officiating roles would have nothing at all to do with gender. This would allow for a person of any sex, gender, identity, and orientation to bring their own dynamic to a role, and express their unique experience in what they do.

Binary gender does not just appear in the officiating roles in traditional Witchcraft. It appears everywhere, from calling elemental quarters, to orienting the altar, to the tools themselves and how they are used. There was no way for us to simply take out binary gender and otherwise keep practicing the same tradition. We needed to create something entirely new.

So we did just that.

The name we chose for our system—*Spectrum Gate Mysteries*—describes some of the fundamental concepts that shape how we go about what we do. "Spectrum" indicated that we were all queer in different ways, and wanted our system to celebrate identity as a spectrum. However, the more we thought about it, the more we realized that the word made sense on a much broader scale. Our entire system is based on an assumption that there are many equally effective and valuable ways of performing ritual. Our system teaches people a spectrum of practice, and encourages them to use whichever works best in each moment.

The term "Gate" emphasizes that the system itself is not the point. The unutterable experience of connection with divinity and with each other is the point. Any ritual system, including ours, is a gateway to that experience. The rituals we perform are meaningful because of where they take us.

Lastly, "Mysteries" signifies that this is a mystery tradition; the experiences we have in ritual are inarticulable in their profundity. We can describe our system, but that's not the same as conveying the meaning of the experience, and that meaning can only truly be understood through the experience itself. Until you have lived that moment yourself, it is a mystery.

Spectrum Gate Mysteries is very clearly composed of pieces far older than we are, yet the way we've put them together is unique. Since we began speaking publicly about what we're doing, we've found other groups across the country that seem to be coming to similar conclusions, and resonate with or even recognize elements of our system in their own. This is wonderful! We invite you to borrow the language here as much or as little as is useful to you. Take what works, and shape it into something that helps you get what you need. Spectrum Gate Mysteries is founded on the idea that spirituality must be adaptable; it must be as diverse as the people that practice it. By its very nature it must be able to change with the ceaseless march of time. Only you can bring yourself to the table, and we want to see what you have to offer.

Coven Craft

Spectrum Gate Mysteries is a type of Coven Craft ... but what is Coven Craft? "Craft" is a term commonly used to describe various forms of Wicca, Witchcraft, and other styles of ritual magic typically aimed at empowerment, transformation, connection with the divine, or some combination thereof. The C in Craft is capitalized to differentiate it from crafts like knitting and woodworking.

A coven is a small dedicated worship group with a formally defined membership. The accountability and intimacy afforded by this type of group creates something essential for intensely personal and meaningful sacred experiences: a common ritual language. Ritual is a language of action. We use ritual to communicate with ourselves, with the Gods, and with each other. The entire point of group ritual of any size is to share our spiritual experiences with each other. Consequently, these rituals are only truly effective when a ritual language is shared among participants.

The bigger your group, the broader your approach will need to be in order to convey meaning to everyone. Sometimes explanations of ritual actions are presented within the ritual itself, often in the form of liturgy or song. At other times, the ritual relies on participants having prior knowledge of that ritual style or tradition. Either way, if that language isn't shared—if people don't understand what the various actions and symbols mean—connections won't happen, and the point of a ritual group is made moot.

A small group with regular members will be able to craft a ritual language ripe with meaning specifically relevant to them and how they work together. Accountability is particularly important here, because people will not want to invest a lot of time and energy learning to speak each other's ritual language if they're not confident that the group will still be around to use it once they all become fluent. It takes time for a group to figure out what type of circle casting they want to use, and it takes practice to learn how to use it effectively.

A group with fewer people can more easily and thoroughly assess the personal spiritual goals of its members and create a ritual system that not only effectively communicates spiritual experiences, but can also be specifically honed to accomplish what its members intend to do. In theory, a group of any size could achieve this level of customization, but the practicalities and logistics of everyday life make it almost impossible for big groups to achieve, whereas it seems to be something that naturally arises in small covens.

Human beings are inherently social creatures. We like having communities; we like sharing our experiences; supporting others and being supported by others. Solitary practice, while important for its own reasons, cannot offer community, or human support. In solitary practice, we explore and develop our private relationships with the divine. In group practice, we share connection with each other, support each other, and explore the human context of spiritual experiences.

Some Pagans try to feed their need for connection by participating in Pagan festivals, regional events, and public rituals, but these don't quite offer the same experience. It is extremely difficult for most people to be vulnerable in the presence of strangers, and the most important moments that happen in a circle require extreme vulnerability. We need safe spaces to do our sacred work, and that doesn't *just* mean properly prepared and warded. It also means space shared with people we can trust, people with whom we can express both our strengths and our weaknesses.

A small group with defined membership can create this type of safe environment in a way that public groups and communities cannot. Limiting the size of a group allows members to invest time and energy into their interpersonal relationships without being burnt out by trying to connect with too many people. It also allows members to carefully craft their group dynamic.

The traditional size limit for a coven is thirteen people, but most large covens seem to "max out" at nine. The logistics of getting thirteen people in the same place at the same time on a regular basis can drive a coordinator to the brink of insanity. Even nine can be challenging. Quite a few covens operate with a core group of just a few members, sometimes numbering only two or three. Many of these groups invite regular guests to some of their rituals—usually friends, partners, or family members; some only ever work with their core members.

Your coven gets to decide how large it will be, and how you want to practice. People who don't quite fit with your coven's attitude or approach do not need to be admitted. Refusing someone's membership doesn't mean that they don't deserve a group at all, nor does it mean they aren't right for any type of Craft. It simply means that your specific group isn't a good fit for them, or that they are not a good fit for your group. You are allowed to set and enforce those boundaries, and doing so will ensure a safer space for all of your members.

Refusals tend to work out best for everyone when the person in question is redirected to other groups with whom they might get along better, or otherwise given whatever resources are available to help them find their own way. An answer of "somewhere, but not here" or "perhaps this other group" is almost always received better than a flat "no". Remember, they may not fit with you, but they still deserve to find their path just as much as anyone else.

Some large Pagan groups and communities offer defined membership, but still don't create the same type of environment one finds in a coven. One reason for this is that accountability works differently in a small group than a large one. When you have thirty people getting together to perform a ritual, having one of them drop out at the last minute is often not a huge problem. There are plenty of other people attending who can take over their responsibilities. Even if they were to be one of the central facilitators of the ritual, a group of thirty often has other qualified individuals who will be ready to step up, and this is one of the strengths of working in a large group. The person who bailed out, however, will often experience no consequences, social or otherwise, for doing so.

This doesn't have to be a bad thing—life often interrupts our best laid plans, and it's good to have a community that is understanding and forgiving. That said, problems arise when the same person drops out at the last minute over and over, but the consequences are little more than a reputation for being flaky. This can be particularly troublesome when the same people are constantly picking up what the flaky person dropped. In my experience, large groups have a very hard time with providing effective consequences for problematic behavior, and the leaders and elders who are always there to help the group cope with those problems burn out alarmingly fast.

In contrast, when you only have three people participating in a ritual, the contributions of each one become absolutely critical. If one person bails out at the last second, everyone has to scramble to cover their role, if the ritual proceeds as planned at all. Everyone feels the impact on the group, and everyone remembers who dropped the ball, and what it took to pick it up again. Consequences become immediately palpable for everyone in a small group, and the effect this has on the members is profound. People are more likely to notify others in advance if something unexpected comes up so that everyone is better able to adapt. Sometimes groups will reschedule to accommodate the member who can't make it, sometimes they cancel, and sometimes they continue as planned. If it happens rarely, or occurrences are evenly distributed amongst group members, an attitude of understanding and support helps the group weather stormy schedules.

If the same person consistently drops out or asks for a schedule change, both they and the group will swiftly feel the consequences. Sometimes a group will simply stop accommodating that person, meaning that they miss out on many rituals and must reassess for themselves how important a coven experience is to them. Often a group will gradually reduce the roles and responsibilities entrusted to that person, as they have shown themselves unable to handle them. Sometimes this is done intentionally, in which case I highly recommend the group be up-front with that person about what is going on and why. Sometimes it happens naturally, as group members assign duties to others they trust to fulfill them, and the flaky person is just never one of those.

Eventually, that person must decide either to invest more of themselves in the group, or accept a marginal role. Likewise, the group must decide if they are comfortable with having a member at the margins. There are many groups who are, and have certain individuals who are not quite members, but are still more than just guests. It is also reasonable for a group to urge that person to seek their sacred elsewhere.

Inclusivity

Many aspects of traditional Wicca and Witchcraft are perfectly useful to anyone of any identity, but they are entrenched in a binary system that limits accessibility. Only those who are comfortable practicing binary ritual will be able to tolerate the system long enough to get access to those universally useful elements of Witchcraft. Spectrum Gate Mysteries presents those elements in a new context where binary polarity is one dynamic amongst many that are equally represented, while retaining magic and ritual elements from traditional Wicca. In doing so, it creates a more *inclusive* coven Craft

The concept of inclusivity for our system started out being about Queerness, and in many ways for our coven it still is. However, inclusivity requires adaptability, and we hope our flexible approach to ritual will open countless possibilities as time ceaselessly demands change. Issues of sex, gender, orientation, and presentation are at the forefront of Pagan discussion now, but what about the future? Modern technology, climate change, and perhaps even interplanetary travel could all push us to adapt our spiritual, magical, and religious practice. The inherent adaptability of inclusive practice can offer solutions for challenges we haven't even imagined yet.

Whether you're a Queer person looking for a system that reflects your non-binary identity, or a binary-gendered person who wants a dynamically inclusive approach to ritual, the tools and techniques offered in this book present an avenue of access to divine experience. You don't have to be Queer enough, or Queer at all, to use this approach to the Craft. Inclusivity means that whoever, whatever, and wherever you are now, you are welcome. You have worth and power. We value what you bring to the table. Our gate might challenge you to recognize and embrace your true self, but it will open for that truth when you find it. Whoever you are, we welcome you to take a step through our gate.

(For interesting reading about the first gay Pagans to challenge the heterosexual bias of the newly-forming Wiccan revival, check out the book Bull of Heaven: The Mythic Life of Eddie Buczynski and the Rise of the New York Pagan, *Michael Lloyd, Asphodel Press, 2012.)*

Terminology

Language can be tricky to navigate in both the Queer and Pagan communities, particularly when we strive to be both semantically inclusive and clearly understood. Various terms can be defined differently based on community, region, tradition, and even personal philosophy. Each of the terms used in this book may be used differently by others, but for the purpose of clear communication, it is important to clarify how a few words are defined.

"Queer" is a word used in this book in a broadly inclusive way. Being Queer can refer to sex, orientation, gender, identity, or any combination thereof. Certain groups might use "Queer" to refer only to those whose gender identity is other than cis-normative, while others use "Queer" to refer to those whose sexual orientation is anything other than heterosexual, or even use the term when referring to a political framework. When these groups collide without taking time to clarify what they mean by "Queer", semantic confusion creates arguments about who does or doesn't qualify as "Queer" enough. Genderqueer people have a right to spaces of their own, as do people with Queer orientation, but I don't really think either would want to deny that of the other. We are all still figuring out how to talk about what we are, and we must be careful not to let language hurt us more than it helps us.

"Trans" is another term that is defined differently in varying communities. Originally used to refer to a change of gender identity (as in "transgender" and "transsexual"), for some of us "Trans" is now more of an umbrella term, encompassing many identity perspectives, while others stick closer to the older definition. In fact, some of the Trans people I interviewed for this book insisted that I too qualify as Trans, while others rejected such a notion. Some Trans people I spoke with felt that a broad definition of "Trans" would appropriate necessary terminology from an already oppressed group, while others felt that a narrow definition of "Trans" would marginalize and trivialize the experiences of people already struggling to be heard.

As I do not choose to identify myself as Trans, I do not feel it is my place to decide who qualifies for the term. However, I do want both this text and the system it describes to be as inclusive and as accessible as possible. Thus, just like the term "Queer", I use the word "Trans" broadly in this book. Here I use it to describe people whose identity has transitioned in some way over the course of their life. This could mean recognizing an identity that has always been present, and transitioning presentation to match that identity, or it could mean a shift in identity itself. I do not claim that this is the only correct definition, but for the sake of clarity it is the only one I will use here. If your take on the term differs, kindly bear with me.

I capitalize the Q in "Queer" and the T in "Trans" to show that I use the words with respect, never as derogatory terms. This is not true for everyone, so if either word bothers you, please feel free to mentally substitute descriptors of your choice.

The terms "Neopagan" and "Pagan" are often used synonymously in our modern Pagan community. "Pagan" can refer to a practitioner of non-Judeo-Christian religion at any point in time, from the farthest reaches of antiquity to the present. "Neopagan" refers to practitioners of contemporary Paganism rather than ancient Paganism, although context generally clarifies whether we're talking about modern or historical Pagans, so I generally tend to choose either Pagan or Neopagan for purely stylistic purposes.

"Witchcraft" is another reclaimed word, much like "Pagan". Pagan Witchcraft is magic (see p. 108) of some sort typically practiced within a spiritual or religious context. There are many types of modern witchcraft, but they are not all Pagan. The W in Witchcraft is capitalized here to dif-

The word Pagan comes from the Latin *paganus,* which meant 'country dweller.' As city dwellers in medieval Europe began to convert to Christianity, rural residents resisted, maintaining their ancient traditions and religions. Urban Christians began to use 'pagans' as a derogatory term to describe these non-Christian countryfolk. Up until very recently, some writers in western academia, heavily influenced by Christianity, would refer to any non-Judeo-Christian person as a Pagan, from tribal peoples in Africa to Buddhist monks in China.

Our contemporary use of Pagan and Neopagan is largely attributed to Oberon Zell-Ravenheart. In the mid-1960s he published a magazine called *Green Egg,* and in it used both 'Pagan' and 'Neopagan' to describe expanding forms of Earth-based spirituality.

ferentiate Pagan Witchcraft from these other types, as well as various forms of witchcraft referenced in anthropology, folklore, and pop culture.

Traditional Wicca is a religion that publicly emerged in its modern form in the mid 1950s. It is initiatory, meaning that one can only become a Traditional Wiccan by undergoing an initiation ritual officiated by a qualified initiate. It is also oathbound, meaning that at least some elements of its rituals are kept secret, known only to initiates. Initiation into Traditional Wicca means entering the priesthood of the Goddess and God of the Witches, although interpretation and identification of this Goddess and God can vary by tradition and sometimes even by coven. Today there are many different traditions of Wicca, as well as some types of Wicca that no longer identify as traditional or keep with traditional practices. Countless books have been written about Wicca in its many forms.

There is still some controversy over whether Gerald Gardner discovered modern Wicca or created it, but there can be no doubt that he was responsible for its proliferation. The Gardnerian Tradition, widely regarded as the oldest form of modern Wicca, takes its name Gerald Gardner. For further information on the history of British Traditional Wicca, see Doreen Valiente's *The Rebirth of Witchcraft* (Robert Hale Ltd, 1998) and Michael Howard's *Modern Wicca: A History From Gerald Gardner to the Present* (Llewellyn Press 2005). For further reading on Wicca in general, see Gerald Gardner's *Witchcraft Today* (Citadel Press, 2004, reprinted from 1956), and *The Meaning of Witchcraft* (Weiser Press 2004, reprinted from 1959); Janet and Stewart Farrar's *A Witches' Bible: The Complete Witches' Handbook* (Phoenix 1996); Starhawk's *The Spiral Dance* (HarperOne 1999); Scott Cunningham's *Wicca: A Guide for the Solitary Practitioner* (Llewellyn Press 1989) and *Living Wicca* (Llewellyn Press 2002); Judy Harrow's *Wicca Covens: How to Start and Organize Your Own* (Citadel Press 1999); and Thea Sabin's *Wicca for Beginners* (Llewellyn Press 2006).

(As you read this book, some of you may feel that what we practice is just another type of Wicca, and that our separation from that term is little more than semantics. That's fine. We are not overly concerned with what other people call us. We know, however, that traditional Wiccans, and especially British Traditional Wiccans, may say that we have changed too much; that our practice could perhaps be called Witchcraft, but it is certainly not Wicca. Out of respect for them, we choose not to use the term Wicca to refer to ourselves.)

The term "circle" has two definitions in this book. On the one hand, it can refer to the physical space that has been warded for a magical rite. (For example, a circle should be large enough to fit your entire group, your altar, and enough room to do whatever sacred work you have planned for your ritual.) On the other hand, it can also describe the entire ritual of creating that space, doing sacred work within it, and deconstructing it afterward. (For example, covens often benefit from making time for purely social interactions outside of circle.)

I use the words "God" and "Gods" as gender-neutral terms. As far as I can tell, the word God started out as gender-neutral, and predates the word Goddess by about a thousand years. There's also a feminist in me that resents the idea that a female divinity has to be a Goddess and not a God. To me the words feel similar to the terms "hunter" and "huntress"; the Latin suffix makes huntress a feminine word, but are we really going to say that women can't be hunters? It seems to me that the suffix was added in a time when female hunters were socially exceptional, and if we want to normalize equity independent of gender, reclaiming words like "God" and "hunter" as gender-neutral terms is part of the work ahead. That said, sometimes gender-affirming language can be incredibly powerful, so the solution may not be throwing out gendered words wholesale. I still use both huntress and Goddess as feminine terms, but use hunter and God as gender neutral terms.

Some people use the term "deity" as a gender-neutral alternative to "God" and "Goddess". I use both terms based on the sense of familiarity being conveyed in the book. For me, there is something personal about the words "God", "Goddess", and "Gods", something definite and known, implying a connection or a level of certainty. Consequently, "God", "Goddess", or "Gods" with the definite article, are used in the book when referencing specific entities, or when there is an implied connection or established relationship. Meanwhile, I use "deities" without the definite article when I want to be intentionally vague about which entities I might be referring to, or when I want to emphasize a lack of familiarity. When referring to a God or the Gods with pronouns, I capitalize the pronoun. This is an expression of my personal reverence, my faith in and respect for Them.

Pagan Fundamentals

Spectrum Gate Mysteries is both spiritual and religious (although it's worth noting that the difference between spirituality and religion can be merely semantic to some, while it's night and day to others). Theoretically it could be adapted for strictly magical use, but one would at the very least need to have a respect for the inherent power of nature in order to use the system effectively. SGM values the sacredness of the land we live on in a way which is integral to its function. Without it, the fundamental premise of our ritual language crumbles.

This Earth-based focus is the most unifying feature of modern Paganism. With the exception of a few who feel they need not embrace the ways in which their Gods are inevitably interconnected with the natural world, there is little Neopagans agree on more readily or unanimously than that nature is sacred. Not all modern Pagans put this concept at the forefront of their worship, but its influence is arguably the most unifying feature of modern Paganism.

A more specific locational awareness goes hand in hand with belief in the sacredness of the Earth. This can manifest in emphasis placed on local landmarks, regional customs inspired by availability or scarcity of natural resources, or the observation of solar cycles. For example, Neopagans in the northern hemisphere celebrate solar holidays at different times than Neopagans in the southern hemisphere because their seasonal cycles are inverted from one another. Similarly, many Neopagans ritually honor specific local seasonal changes, or celebrate common solar holidays in ways that are relevant to their area. In general, the localized observation of solar and lunar cycles is common in most forms of Neopaganism. Pagan Sabbats (see page 80) and Wicca-inspired moon magic is only one way these cycles find their way into modern Paganism. Many ancient calendars used by modern polytheists are based on both solar and lunar cycles as well.

The four elements of fire, air, water, and earth are another tremendously common feature of modern western Paganism. Sometimes spirit is added to these as a fifth element, and sometimes the same group will work with four elements in some contexts and five elements in others. The four elements have a long history in western philosophy and magic, dating back at least as far as Plato's *Timaios* from 360 B.C.E.

In Traditional Wicca each elements corresponds with both a gender and a cardinal direction—male fire in the south, male air in the east, female water in the west, and female earth in the north—but these associations did not sit well with our group. To begin with, we can find both male, female and other-gendered energy in every element, so limiting any element to a single gender made no sense to us. Furthermore, for all that the cardinal directions have their historical associations with each element (which, by the way, are not at all as universal as some Neopagans might like to think, even just within western Europe), we are based on the east coast of America. We occasionally perform ritual on the beach, and we felt tremendously silly calling upon elemental water with our backs to the ocean. The elements remain an integral part of the SGM ritual system, but we've devised a way of working with them that emphasizes locational awareness, and allows any gender or none to manifest within each element.

No overview of Neopagan fundamentals would be complete without some mention of energy. If you put nine Pagans together in a room and ask them what energy is, you'll get at least thirteen different definitions. Some common descriptions include:

❖ the essence of spirit, the fifth element
❖ the metaphysical counterpart of physical reality
❖ a way to describe the energy of which our atoms are composed
❖ the "stuff" of spiritual reality, with physical reality and spiritual as interconnected yet separate worlds

The one thing most Pagans *are* likely to agree on is that, in some way or another, energy exists, and we can affect it. Neopagan ritual and magic is built upon concepts of raising, manipulating, and directing energy, so whatever you think it is or isn't, you'll need some sort of belief in its existence in order for SGM to be useful to you.

Finally, there is one more philosophical concept which I would like to emphasize. As a principle it is certainly not unique to our group, but it has become our most fundamental value: think for yourself. Learn as much as you can so that your decisions are well informed, but make up your own mind.

Don't do things exactly as I describe them just because I wrote it that way. Think about these ideas, compare them with your knowledge base and your experience, and decide what you want or need to do.

Act consciously in accordance with your own needs. Do what you must do in order to be at peace with yourself. No one can decide that for you, so educate yourself, and think.

Our entire system is built on the idea that people will gather information about possible ways ritual can be done, and then decide in each moment which option is most appropriate, or create a new way if nothing known seems to work. Adapt. Innovate. Create. Cultivate awareness, and think for yourself.

Creating Sacred Space

What Is Sacred Space?

Any time we want to seriously engage in an activity, it helps to have a place specifically dedicated to it. Writers often have a place they go to write, artists sometimes have a studio arrayed with tools they use to create, and many athletes have a gym or track or pool they train in. Being in these special places both tells the person on a psychological level that it is now time to engage in that activity, putting them in an optimal mindset for the task at hand, and gives them the physical things they need to work most efficiently. Consecrating space with a circle accomplishes these same things: it puts ritual participants in a headspace that is conducive to their purpose, while also providing energetic and physical tools that will facilitate their work.

Performing this work in protected space means that participants can hone their focus on the task at hand. Again, this is something we do with many mundane activities as well: the writer turns off their phone when it's time to write; the artist locks the front door and puts on music while they paint; the basketball player swipes their membership card as they enter the gym, thus knowing that only other members will be able to get in. Each of these theoretical people are placing themselves in an environment where their work will not be interrupted, and they will be surrounded only by others present for the same reason.

In circle we create this same type of protection for ourselves. The sphere of energy we create is like the walls of a house with doors we can lock and unlock at will. We can invite guardian spirits to sit at the doorways we create, acting like the receptionist at the gym making sure everyone has their membership card. We can set our intent in the circle casting and let that energy charge our work, like letting music inspire a painting. This atmosphere of dedicated safety allows participants to reveal themselves in ways that they can't when they're on guard in an unfamiliar setting, or watching out for potential interruptions, or constantly refocusing their energy. That vulnerability allows us to engage with our spirituality more fully, achieve our goals with better clarity, and transform ourselves in accordance with our will.

Why A Circle?

Before we even begin to talk about how to cast a circle, we need to understand why we might want a *circle* in the first place.

I mentioned above that my upline—the ritual system I was trained and initiated in—happens to be traditional Wicca, but it's also worth noting that I consider myself to be at my core a polypraxic polytheist. The polytheist part means that I believe there are many different deities with independent agency. The polypraxic part means that I practice a number of different traditions rather than exclusively devoting myself to any single one.

I do not believe that there is any "right" way to "do" religion or spirituality. I believe that each person must determine what is "right" for them, and that "right" for even one single person can change in different circumstances. In general, I believe that "right" itself is tremendously subjective. Certainly I have opinions about what is respectful or disrespectful, what should or shouldn't be done, what is or isn't appropriate worship for certain deities, but I also believe that I am a mortal being with only as much insight as a mortal brain can hold. I cannot possibly know all of what is right or wrong for everyone. At the end of the day, the determination of what you need to do is between you and the Gods (or divinity in whatever form you perceive it). While I do not believe They know everything, I certainly believe They understand a lot more than me.

Many books on modern Wicca, Witchcraft, and other forms of Coven Craft seem to carry with them an assumption that casting a circle is the thing to do, but don't examine any reasoning behind that assumption. When I was standing in circle and feeling its effect, that experience was enough. As I began to create Spectrum Gate Mysteries, however, I wanted more, both for myself and for others who would someday practice our system. I wanted to be able to articulate not just *how* circles provide people with a profound sacred experience, but also *why* circles are such a good way to go about it. I needed to understand why I, or anyone else, would bother casting a circle at all. So what is a circle, and why is it useful? What's it all for?

A circle is a consecrated and warded space in which sacred, magical, or spiritual work can be accomplished. It's a physical area that is specially dedicated to your intent, and protected against interference. "Casting a circle" refers to the process by which said space is designated, dedicated and protected. In essence, a circle is a sort of hybrid between a spatial consecration and a ward. Circles are not meant to be permanent installations. They are transient constructs of energy and intent, created when they are required and disassembled or dispersed once they have served their purpose.

Consequently, while casting a circle can seem somewhat overly complex at first, a coven that regularly practices casting and dispersing in their chosen format will find that it offers great utility. It can be cast anywhere the group can fit themselves, and leaves no trace when properly dispersed. Once everyone gets the hang of the ritual system, the process of creating sacred space becomes natural. It no longer requires conscious thought, but flows freely as an inarticulate expression of energy, community, and intent. What once seemed unnecessarily complex becomes instead a shared language fluently spoken. This allows everyone participating to deepen their connection to one another, and enhance their focus on the reason they created that space in the first place. The end result is a generally more immersive experience.

Ritual Tools

My former teacher once confided in me that they always felt rather silly marching off into the woods with a huge bag of ritual gear to do circle. It seemed to them that one ought to be able to work magic amongst the trees with nothing but their own self, but they felt pressured by their tradition to keep all the bells and whistles even while surrounded by nature's own raw magic.

Of course, there is some truth in both perspectives. Many magicians and ritualists concur that an individual's Will is the key to magic, and ritual tools serve only to direct that Will. To be sure, a skilled occultist can raise tremendous power naked and alone, wielding nothing more and nothing less than their own mind, body, and spirit.

That said, Coven Craft, at least as it persists today in a broadly Neopagan sense, is meant to be accessible to anyone with a genuine desire to participate. As much as we would all love to fancy ourselves masters of the arcane arts, some people just don't perceive energy very well, let alone direct it, and it is my belief that the Craft should be just as welcoming to them as to the person who can charge a spell just as easily as they write their name. This is a huge part of what makes ritual tools so important: they help people move energy and perform acts of ritual and magic even if they don't have a great natural sense of what they're doing.

While utility is certainly the biggest reason for keeping ritual tools as part of your practice, it's certainly not the only reason. Many covens begin training new students by teaching the various attributes and functions of the ritual tools they use. From an educational perspective, this allows students to engage in a variety of different learning styles according to their strengths, whether it's making lists of relevant properties, feeling the weight and texture of different tools, or seeing and practicing how tools are used in circle.

Finally, the very reason that ritual tools make such solid multidimensional teaching tools is that they tend to reflect the group's approach to both ritual and magic. A group with a strong ethic of nonviolence is unlikely to have any sort of ritual blade, instead putting more emphasis on a sacred mirror for reflection and introspection, or consecrated dishware for bonding through shared meals.

Ritual tools are a physical piece of ritual language, and as such Spectrum Gate Mysteries has a set of standard tools that comprise our default altar setup. We describe this setup as "default" because the altar and its tools can and should change in accordance with our circumstances, accommodating everything from physical space to magical intent. Learning and practicing a "default" allows us to establish points of commonality in our ritual language, so that when we do modify our practice, we still have enough touchstones of familiarity to effectively communicate.

Most of our tools are common features of Pagan practice, and we intentionally tap into the legacy of their traditional use. The concept of attribute and function that goes along with an item, particularly when based on the inherent properties of that item, takes on a power of its own which is amplified by everyone who partakes in it. We want to access that power when it fits within the broader view of our system, but we also expand the possibilities for each tool by including opportunity for practice outside a binary and polar dynamic. Some familiar tools find new interpretation and use in Spectrum Gate Mysteries.

Each of the four elements—fire, air, water, and earth—have both a tool and a representative on the altar, the tool being more metaphorical and utilitarian, while the representative is as literal as possible. These elemental tools and representatives are also called the quarter tools, as we place them in the four quarters of the altar. We also have cross-quarter tools, implements that are not associated with a single element, but reflect the energetic interplay between elements. Finally, some ritual implements are neither quarter nor cross-quarter tools, and their function determines their placement in circle.

The Athame

The athame or ritual knife is our quarter tool of air, associated with thought and knowledge. Its blade is sharp because we want our minds to be precise and discerning; it is double-edged because facts are impartial and knowledge can cut both ways, and it is reflective because we must ever be aware of how our own biases affect our thinking. The blade is ferrous because iron has a long history of being used to dispel and defend against unwanted magic, and steel because the practice and discipline of forging quality steel that will hold an edge over time speaks to us of collecting significant quantities of relevant data to create a well-informed opinion. Just as even the best steel knives must occasionally be sharpened, so to must we continuously educate ourselves to maintain a mental edge.

In circle the athame is used both to direct and disperse energy. The handle is made from a non-conductive material painted black, a color that both protects and absorbs. This combination creates a sort of unidirectional valve, allowing the wielder to push energy through the athame and outward, while simultaneously being insulated from whatever the tool comes into contact with.

Aside from its sheer utility, the athame also stands as a warning to anyone or anything that might attempt to interfere with our work. When we greet deities and spirits by openly baring our weapons, we declare that our intent is not to deceive, yet we also declare that we are not defenseless. Our Spectrum Gate leads to empowerment, and our blades are symbols of that power.

The selection of an athame is an intensely personal process, and teaches some important general lessons about tool sourcing. Traditional attributes—for example, a shiny, double-edged blade—are worth considering for their symbolism and function, but at the end of the day you're the one who has to wield the tool in sacred space, so the most important attributes are those that speak to you personally. Some people enjoy tapping into the power of traditional form, while others want implements that reflect their own unique personality. Knowing what and why those traditional qualities are—for example, why that double edged blade is supposed to be shiny—helps you make your own decisions about what kind of tool you want.

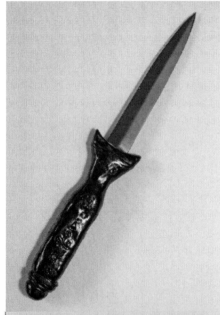

The author's Athame, made from a discarded blade, and repurposed with an oven-bake polymer clay handle.

Today it is too easy to find cheaply made mass-produced ritual tools for sale. The manufacturing and shipping of these items have an environmental impact that we, as practitioners of an Earth-based spiritual system, ought to avoid. We don't need to buy our tools; we can make them, either from raw materials or by "upcycling" other objects. Even an athame can be made by repurposing an old knife; make a new handle out of wood or clay, and decorate it with symbols and sigils that have meaning to you. The energy and effort we put into making or refurbishing a ritual tool adds to the power of that implement.

Of course, some of us just aren't the crafty type, and that's OK. Consider buying your ritual tools from a craft fair, from a store that offers ethically sourced fair trade items, or from a local artist or craftsperson. Many freelance artists have websites where they sell their creations. If you can't find anything that suits you nearby, support our community by buying your tools from Queer crafters.

Consecrating or blessing an athame can be as elaborate or as simple as you like. Sometimes an object used in ritual because it's what happened to be on hand at the time becomes a consecrated ritual tool because of the sacred energy imbued in it during that ritual. If you have a fancy dagger you like to use at SCA events, for example, think twice before you use it for ritual, because you might find yourself unable to use it for anything else afterward! A very simple consecration involves sprinkling the tool with saltwater and passing it through incense smoke, thus imbuing it with the energy of each of the four elements. Add a prayer, dedication, or declaration of intent to customize that tool for yourself and your purposes.

Ritual knives have a rich history in magic around the world. The word "athame" most likely comes from the medieval Latin word *artavus* meaning "small knife", which was later corrupted in French and Italian translations of the Key of Solomon. Ceremonial magicians use a ritual knife they call an athame, as do traditional Wiccans. The athame of traditional Wicca was almost certainly influenced by the Malaysian *kris,* a blade that is both a weapon and a ceremonial dagger. While living on a rubber plantation he owned in Malaya, Gerald Gardner befriended an American man named Cornwall, who introduced Gardner to various indigenous people who shared with him some of their beliefs and practices. Gardner would later practice what is now called British Traditional Wicca.

The Wand

The wand is even more well-known than the athame, appearing in folklore and mythology from around the world, taking different forms from the elaborate rod decorated with precious metals and gemstones to a simple stick found on a walk through the woods.

The wand is our quarter tool of fire, associated with Will and action. It is a conduit for energy, used to direct power in magic and ritual. Its shape helps the wielder feel power emanating from themselves, and helps them visualize the direction the energy travels in. The material of which the wand is made can intensify, focus, diversify, homogenize, and otherwise manipulate the energy pushed through it.

We prefer a natural wooden wand, as plants grow nourished by the fires of the Sun, and wood is perhaps the most ancient fuel for fire. We select which wood to use in circle based on its magical properties. Willow, for example, is a popular choice for beginners as it can enhance spiritual connection with an energy that is firm yet gentle. Most books about magical herbs also include information about sacred woods, so for more information look to volumes such as *The Master Book of Herbalism* by Paul Beyerl (1984).

When possible, we prefer to use wood that has already been separated from a tree to use for our wands, as I was taught that the wand should be a gift, and sometimes that "gift" is finding just the wood you need. This might mean finding branches that have naturally broken off a tree, or cutting a piece from a fallen limb. You could also wait for when local parks do their pruning, and taking a branch or two from what they trim. When we cut wood ourselves to craft a wand, perhaps while making a gift for someone else, we take care to cut a piece that will not affect the overall health of the tree, and we leave a small gift for the tree in return for what we take—for example, water or a bit of fertilizer, or some food that won't harm whatever ecosystem we leave it in. Items full of artificial dyes, preservatives, or other additives are generally not a good choice.

Sometimes the piece of wood we find determines the dimensions of the wand. First and foremost, it must feel comfortable in the hand of the person who will wield it, and this is often what makes the "right" piece of wood just right. Sometimes the wood we find is larger than we need, and the work of sanding and carving a wand to just the right size helps us bond to our tool, or

A rowan wand crafted by the author from a branch found fallen after a storm.

invest energy in a gift. Using the dimensions of the wielder's body to de-termine the dimensions of the wand can be another way to enhance that bond. For example, one traditional length for a wooden wand was from the pit of the elbow to the end of the middle finger, with a circumference no larger than the thumb and no narrower than the little finger.

The Cup

The cup is our quarter tool of water, associated with emotion and spiritual nourishment. Once the altar is set, we never allow it to run empty until we give our final toast to the Gods at the end of circle, signifying the boundless nature of love. After the toast, we drain the cup for the Gods, as we devote our whole hearts to the divine. When the cup is empty while setting the altar or after the toast, we place it upside down, turning it into a representation of the hollow void which in its emptiness has infinite po-tential for formation and manifestation.

Our group uses a large ceramic goblet for our ritual cup. It holds enough liquid for each of us to be able to drink during circle, and it feels special to us in a way that is appropriate for ritual use. Large shared ritual cups are a common practice in Wicca-based Paganism, and they can be excellent symbols of shared spiritual sustenance.

That said, if you choose to have a sin-gle ritual goblet, you must have a conver-sation with your group about the inherent health risks of sharing a cup, and make sure that everyone consents before being put on the spot in the middle of ritual. Viruses like flu and cold sores can easily spread by drinking from the same cup, so before you share a cup in circle, talk about what types of risk your group finds ac-ceptable, and what your group wants to avoid. If a member occasionally has cold sores but isn't currently having an outbreak, are people comfortable sharing a cup with them? If someone is sick, should they not

A ritual cup painted by the author at a paint-your-own-pottery store.

drink from a communal cup? If some people are allowed to drink from the group cup but not others, will that bother the people who can't drink? Prior discussion can let everyone make healthy decisions for themselves and their fellow coven members without attracting any unnecessary stigma.

Some groups will let someone make a toast instead of taking a drink and then pass the cup along, and this may well let someone who happens to have a spring cold (for example) feel included despite being unable to drink, but what if there's one member that *never* gets to drink? An alternative is to consecrate a beverage in a pitcher, then pour some into individual cups for every participant. In this way everyone drinks from the same vessel, yet everyone drinks from their own vessel, which speaks to the unique combination of both shared and personal experience individuals find in coven Craft.

I should note that our coven is very small, so conversations about which sort of cup we should use and what risks we are willing to take are significantly less complicated for us than for many others. When we host open rituals with guests, we either use a pitcher and individual cups, or we have a conversation with everyone beforehand about the cup and its use in ritual, making people aware of any potential risks and inviting them to participate by toasting, kissing the outside of the cup, or drinking, as they see fit.

The practice of kissing the outside of the cup and passing it along serves as a useful tool for sober alcoholics wanting to participate in sharing a ritual drink despite the ubiquitous use of alcohol in Wiccan circles. Kissing the outside of the cup allowed them to express reverence and respect for the cup and what it represented to their group while maintaining their sobriety. We find that this is a useful option to offer to guests who are not concerned with sharing germs, but either can't or don't want to drink our selected beverage.

That said, the drink inside the cup or cups can be as important as the vessels themselves. Alcoholic beverages are common for a variety of reasons. The physiological effects of alcohol were likely relevant to older forms of traditional Wicca, where power-raising was often performed with ecstatic dance. The fermentation process means that alcoholic drinks are transformed substances, which makes them appropriate sources of sympathetic power for magic centered around transformation. Some types of alcoholic drinks (mead, for example) still contain living yeast when they are imbibed, and the literal presence of life in the cup is very important to some groups. Of course, the same can be said for freshly squeezed juices, as many cells from the fruit will still be alive when you drink them.

We tend to think first of the deities we will be approaching in circle, and select from beverages amenable to Them. We offer the best of what we have or can acquire, and choose something that everyone present will be able and willing to drink. When we invite guests, we ask about allergies and taboos that would limit what people can ingest, and do our best to select something that will work for everyone. The point of sharing a drink, after all, is to sate our thirst together as a community, in both a physical and spiritual sense.

Salt

Salt's properties as a natural preservative are likely responsible for its widespread history as a magical tool for purification and protection. Salted food would last far longer before spoiling, so salt became associated with protection and cleansing. Many modern traditions, including our own, consider salt to be inherently pure.

Salt is our quarter tool of earth, associated with stability and manifestation. In circle we use salt for purification, protection, and grounding by either physically putting it in contact with something, or ingesting it. Salty foods can be quite helpful for grounding a congregation both during and after ritual.

Today salt is available in a variety of forms, and each one has its own flavor in both a literal and energetic sense. Rock salt harvested from a mine tends to have an earthier taste, and is excellent for magic centered around solidity, manifestation, and foundation. Sea salt tends to work particularly well for purification and emotional stability. We try to avoid iodized salt, but it can still work well for purification, as iodine is used as a disinfectant in

A stone bowl holding salt.

certain circumstances, and there is power in the practicality of using what you've got on hand.

Fresh Water

Most traditional Wiccan, and even most Wiccan-derived, covens have water on their altar, but typically that water gets mixed with salt as part of the circle casting. While the resulting salt water mixture is an important tool in and of itself, our system holds fresh water as equally important and uniquely useful in ritual. Consequently we place both salt water and fresh water on our altar.

Fresh water is our quarter representative of elemental water. Humans need fresh water to sate our thirst, and the earth needs fresh water for life to thrive on it—even in the desert, water is essential. The fresh water on our altar is a symbol of springs, lakes, rivers, rain, and other natural sources of fresh water upon which our survival depends

Part of our attraction to keeping fresh water as a distinct ritual tool is the historical practice of using local water sources to connect to a specific landscape. In ancient Greece, for example, women would carry water from their home to wherever they would get married so that they could take their nuptial bath in their own water as a spiritual connection to the land they were born on. In our modern world, it is too easy to let the wonders of plumbing draw our attention away from where our water comes from and how our location affects what we drink. Ritual fresh water reminds us of our dependence on natural resources.

In circle we use our fresh water for acts of purification in which the emphasis is on connecting to where we are, what we're doing, and the company we keep. Fresh water purification is gentler than salt water; cleansing and preparing while leaving strong energetic bonds intact. We also drink fresh water in acts of magic aimed at strengthening our bonds with the land the water comes from, or empowering ourselves through our connection to that land.

A ceramic bowl received as a hand-made gift from a childhood friend, now used as a ritual water bowl.

Salt Water

Mixing salt and water together combines the attributes of each to create a cross-quarter tool with its own unique utility, cleansing with the power of both salt and water. Gentle yet firm, it insists on purity and fluidly protects. Our ritual salt water is a reference to the ocean, and as such also carries in it the energy of primordial life.

A store-bought black and white bowl with consecrated saltwater.

Our primary use for salt water in ritual is to asperge or sprinkle the mixture around a freshly cast circle. Salt water maintains the fixative properties of salt, so asperging seals the circle, solidifying our energetic ward. A circle of salt alone would offer sturdy protection, but it would be *too* static for the type of sacred space we want: a place where we can welcome and commune with other entities and energies. Energetic walls of salt are extremely difficult to pass through, which makes for strong but insular protection. Mixing salt with water provides us with a solution that is still powerfully protective, yet fluidly adaptable. We can open and close doorways in a circle sealed with salt water, allowing us to create avenues of easy passage for the deities and spirits we want to meet.

The Anchor (the officiator who sets the altar—see pages 51 and 56) begins by placing the tip of an athame in the center of the water and spiraling outward. Then they name three attributes associated with water which we want to exclude from our work—for example, emotional insecurity, jealousy, and clouded intuition. As they name each thing we want to be rid of, they draw it out with the athame and cast it behind them with a vigorous flick of the blade (watch out behind you as you do this, though!). Then they begin to consecrate the water by placing the tip of the athame at the edge of the water and spiraling inward.

When they reach the center, they name three attributes associated with water which we want to emphasize in our work—for example, vulnerability, compassion, and love. As they name each one, they focus on sending that energy into the water through the athame. Next the Anchor consecrates the salt in a similar fashion. Cleansing is unnecessary because salt is inherently pure. The Anchor places the athame at the edge of the salt and spirals inward. At the center they name three attributes associated with salt that we want to emphasize in our work—for example, stability, tradition, and manifestation. Again, as they name each one, they push that energy through the athame and into the salt. Finally, the builder pours some water into a separate container, scoops three lumps of salt into that container, and stirs the mixture three times. We mix our water with words I inherited from the Blue Star Wiccan tradition: "Salt joins with water as lover joins lover, as we would all join with the universe." I encourage you to compose words of your own if these do not resonate with you.

Salt water also finds some use in ritual magic and spellcraft. A "spritz" of salt water can lock a spell or energy construct in place, just as it seals the sphere of our circle. As a symbol of shed tears, salt water can also be a powerful tool for emotional catharsis, allowing someone to "cry" when their body won't. In sympathetic magic (see p. 114) it can be a symbol for sweat, representing hard work and effort put forth towards a goal.

The act of mixing water and salt is often included in process of casting a circle. We chose to make this part of our preparation because we wanted to make sure we put more emphasis on the work we do within circle than on the act of casting circle. Nevertheless, we maintain a fairly traditional method of cleansing, consecrating, and mixing our salt and water, which we perform as we set the altar.

Consecrating your salt water mixture in this way serves a double purpose. For one, this process is part of what makes the salt water such an intensely powerful ritual tool, and the attributes you name during your consecration can fine tune that utility to work with the specific magic or ritual you have planned. Beyond that, however, the process of consecrating the salt water also involves cleansing and consecrating the fresh water. As water does not have the inherent purity of salt, if you choose not to use this method of consecration but still plan to have fresh water on your altar, you should consider an alternative method of cleansing and consecrating your fresh water.

The Bell

A small ritual hand bell.

The bell is the quarter representative of air on our altar. This will doubtless come as a bit of a surprise to my Wiccan colleagues, as the phallic clapper within the hollow bell makes it a symbol of heterosexual sex in traditional Wicca. While it's worth remembering that symbolism as one option for use should the need arise, we decided to focus on different symbolism in the bell as a ritual tool.

In the most technical sense, it is not the bell itself that is our literal representative of air on the altar, but the sound that the bell makes: the vibration of the bell reaches our ears through waves of compressed air. As a tool, the bell calls attention, opens and closes, and facilitates spiritual travel, which we also found appropriate for an association with elemental air. As the ring reaches your ears, your mind focuses on the task at hand, and your spirit moves toward its goal.

Small hand bells tend to make the best ritual bells. A jingle bell can work in a pinch, but there is something about the clear tone of a hand bell—even a tiny, old-fashioned dinner bell—that works particularly well for ritual use. Singing bowls can also work well as a ritual bell, but it can be tough to fit a singing bowl on your altar unless you have a particularly small bell, or a very large altar!

The Stone

Our quarter representative of elemental earth is an actual piece of the Earth, usually a stone. Stones have great utility as ritual tools, as their weight and solidity have a naturally grounding effect, particularly when they are fist-sized or larger. You could use a local stone you find in or near the area you plan to cast your circle to deepen the connection between your ritual and the land you're on. You could select a semiprecious gemstone for each circle with magical properties that will enhance the work you have planned. Your group could select a stone together and charge it (see page 109) with community and continuity, so that it becomes not only a representative of elemental earth and a grounding tool, but also a symbol of your group's stability and longevity.

Tons of resources exist explaining the magical properties of different types of stones. My favorite remains *Cunningham's Encyclopedia of Crystal, Gem, and Metal Magic* by Scott Cunningham (Llewellyn Press, 1996); you can also look at *Crystal Power, Crystal Healing* (Michael Gienger, Cassel Illustrated, 2015). Remember that river stones and beach stones also have unique properties worth considering, as do the rocks you dig up while tending a garden, or the pebbles you find on a hike. While semiprecious gems can certainly be useful, you don't always have to go straight to your local crystal shop to get a ritual stone. If you do buy a stone online or at a local store, be sure to cleanse it before you put it on your altar or use it in circle. Let it sit in a bowl of salt for a few days, or wash it with consecrated saltwater.

Sometimes we have need for dirt in our magic, and when we do, we let the dirt be our representative of earth. Soil can be charged with energy and used for rituals involving themes such as planting, growth, and fertility. While less obviously grounding than a heavy stone, dirt absorbs energy quite well, and can still help someone shed their excess if they find themselves overwhelmed during circle.

Candles

Candles appear in a few different places on our altar. We use a flame as our quarter representative of elemental fire, typically with either a red votive candle or a tea light candle in a red candle holder. When we need to burn something in ritual with the transformative energy of elemental fire, we light it from the fire candle.

We also have a candle lit for each deity we intend to call upon during ritual. Being the polytheists that we are, we reach out to at least one deity in every circle, but no more than three at a time, as we feel that we cannot give proper attention to any more than that. I should note, however, that I have both witnessed and participated in rituals that included many more than three deities at once, although all of these involved more participants than we have in our coven. Large rituals with many deities can work, so long as you have enough officiators to ensure that each are honored appropriately—and "enough" can change depending on Who you're working with!

At the very center of our altar, we place a plain white candle representing what we refer to as The Source. To us it is a reminder that divinity at its most fundamental level is something incomprehensibly vast, so profound that it cannot be adequately described, only referenced to. It is a reminder that we are all connected somehow, and we feel that connection even if we struggle to articulate it, or articulate it in different ways. Some might call it the Wyrd, or the web of fate, or describe it as a tangled combination of animism and immanence. Perhaps you will describe it differently, or go without it entirely, but I suggest you try it at least once. There is something inarticulably powerful about having a symbol of divine connection at the very center of the altar.

Incense

Incense is another substance with a long history of ritual use, and finds a place on our altar as a cross-quarter tool, typically between air and fire. Smoke rising to the heavens is an ancient form of offering to the Gods, and different types of incense can have a purifying, sanctifying, consecrating, and even intensifying effect on your magic or ritual. Our sense of smell is deeply linked to our emotional and mental states, so the scent of incense can help participants shift to a spiritual mindset.

A censer found at a yard sale, accompanied by loose incense made by the author.

As incense is generally made from a combination of plants, oils, and resins, books on herbalism can give you excellent insight into which types of incense are good for which occasions. My favorites include *The Master Book of Herbalism* by Paul Beyerl (1984), and *Cunningham's Encyclopedia of Magical Herbs* by Scott Cunningham (1985). If you need a solid option to get started, frankincense and sandalwood each make good choices for most purposes and are easy to find, but I encourage you to research your options and select the incense that will best suit your intent.

You can buy incense pre-made as sticks or cones, or you can select the specific herbs, oils, and resins you want to use, mix them together, and burn them on incense charcoal. Stick incense comes in two different varieties: cored sticks or solid cylinders. Solid cylinders are either thick, hand-rolled sticks, or thin sticks made a bit like spaghetti. Cored sticks have a reed core, and are made by dipping or rolling the reed in paste or dough. Some cheaply made cored incense sticks use industrial glues that are toxic when burned, and are dangerous in enclosed areas. If you want to use stick incense in ritual, research different brands, and make sure the type you buy is appropriate for your space, your health, and the environment.

Stick incense can be burned on a long, narrow incense burner of the sort that has small holes in which you insert the stick. Some types of incense come with tiny tiles with a hole in the center that also work well for that purpose. Special burners can also be found for cone incense, usually metal or ceramic with bottoms that encourage air circulation, but a small heat resistant plate can work just as well. Loose incense and charcoal can be burned in a censer, which usually has the added benefit of a chain or handle by which you can carry the burning charcoal and incense around your circle.

You don't necessarily need to go out and buy fancy equipment for your incense. A bowl filled with dirt, salt, or ash can be a perfectly good holder for stick or cone incense, as well as a perfectly serviceable censer. Just make sure that you use a heat-resistant bowl, and that you have enough dirt, salt, or ash in it to keep the bowl from heating up too much to touch. We use a mixture of salt and ash, which insulates well while keeping the charcoal well aerated.

Food

The Craft is concerned not only with matters of mind and spirit, but of body as well. As such, food is a cross-quarter tool on our altar, representing visceral life and physical sustenance. Sharing food is a way for people to bond as a community by literally nourishing each other. In offering our food to the Gods as well, we express reverence to Them, include Them in our community, and include ourselves in Theirs.

Ritually consecrating and consuming food in circle helps us re-center our focus on our bodies after flying high on the intense energies of ritual. Eating is naturally grounding, which typically shuts down high energy states. Because the food shared in circle is imbued with energy in its consecration, and usually falls short of a full meal, being more like a snack or a token portion, sharing ritual food eases the energetic buzz rather than killing it altogether. It offers people a gentler way to transition from a fully heightened energetic state to practical mundane awareness.

Eating can also be a way to bring our magic into our physical forms—food becomes a part of us as we eat it, so if we imbue our food with specific energies, perhaps even using ingredients associated with those qualities, we then bring those attributes into ourselves in a very literal way. Magical cooking is its own discipline, combining elements of herbalism spellcraft, and sympathetic magic. Additives can create or enhance the magical properties of ritual foods, and can include anything from baked in charms (which you must be careful not to swallow accidentally), to sacred herbs grown for a particular purpose, to the bodily fluids of the practitioner.

As with the drink we put in the cup, we try to select food to share in circle that is amenable to the deities we call on, safe for everyone to consume, and the best of what we have to offer. Charles Leland's *Aradia, or the Gospel of the Witches* (David Nutt Ltd. 1899) mentioned cakes made from salt, meal, honey, and wine, which still serves as the basic recipe for many traditional witches and Wiccans. Sometimes we too pay our tribute to tradition, but sometimes we use fruit, nuts, cheese, pastries, bread, or anything else at all that is appropriate for the circle we have planned.

After the circle is closed, sharing a full communal meal is a good idea, allowing everyone to solidify their transition to mundane awareness. This also gives the group time for social bonding in a more relaxed environment, where any kind of conversation is welcome.

The Libation Bowl

A libation is an offering of drink poured out to a deity, although in some communities within modern Paganism, people also use the term libation to refer to food offerings. As discussed above, the food and drink shared in circle is not just meant for us, but for the Gods as well. Thus, we offer a portion of both food and drink to the deities called upon during ritual. While outdoors, this portion can be poured directly onto the ground, or left in some discreet place. Some Pagans believe that the animals who come to eat food offerings left behind are acting as agents of the Gods, and a few even take omens from which animals come to collect.

That said, indoor rituals necessitate somewhere to put the portions allotted to the Gods, and even during outdoor rituals leaving food and drink offerings can be unwise. For example, grapes are extremely toxic to dogs, so if you cast your circle in a park where people often walk their dogs and use grapes as your food in circle, you'll want to make sure you take them with you when you leave, and find some other place to set them out for the Gods. In these sorts of situations, a libation bowl is the obvious solution. We not only place the Gods' portion of food and drink in the bowl, but also let anyone who wishes to do so add a little bit of their own portion as an extra offering.

Sometimes people don't have an outdoor space to leave their food, or don't want to put their libations outside because of the animals or insects it might attract. In this case you can leave the food on an altar indoors overnight, with the intent that the Gods will take from it the spirit of the substance, and what remains the next day can simply be disposed of. If you're lucky enough to have access to a fireplace or fire pit, you could burn your libations during or after circle.

That said, even when we cast circles in places where we can easily distribute our offerings, we still choose to include a libation bowl as a cross-quarter tool. We collect food and drink offerings within the bowl, and deliver them from there once the ritual is finished. The libation bowl is a symbol as well as a tool; it represents sacrifice and gratitude, the fact that we must work for what we want, and the idea that our relationship with the Gods thrives on exchange, not just begging for what we want. When we place the libation bowl full of offerings on our altar, we make a statement that we are thankful for what we have, that we are willing to give for what we want, and that we recognize and embrace the interconnectedness of all of us in how the sacrifice of one can nourish another, and the nourishment of one can be a sacrifice for another.

When we feast together after ritual, we bring the libation bowl with us, and add a tiny portion from each dish into the bowl. This helps connect our meal outside of circle to our ritual actions within circle, and it shows that our commitment to exchange and gratitude persists even when we've left sacred space.

The Scourge

The scourge is a cross-quarter tool representing discipline and endurance. Ritual flagellation can be seen as a sort of counterpoint to the sacred meal. Both are concerned with the sacred potential of physical experience, but while ritual food and drink brings us nourishment and pleasure, scourging brings us insight gained through suffering.

Pain applied skillfully, intentionally, consensually, and non-injuriously can be a powerful tool for personal revelation and transformation. Physiological responses to pain can help us break out of old mental habits, and inducing that state in a carefully crafted ritual atmosphere can let us replace self-destructive patterns with constructive thinking and new potential. The scourge has become the most common tool for sacred pain in modern Witchcraft because of its use in Traditional Wicca, but any type of physical suffering can be used to the same effect. The Ordeal path of power (see p. 117) extends this concept to embrace the transformational possibilities of non-physical suffering as well.

A ritual scourge handcrafted by the author resting atop a mirror purchased at a craft store.

Learning to wield pain ethically is a skill that requires practice and discipline; thus, the scourge becomes a symbol not only of sacred ordeals, but also of discipline itself. It reminds us that we must balance indulgence with self-control, and that with power comes the necessary burden of conscious choice.

The Mirror

Mirrors are well-known in mythology, folklore, and various traditions as tools for divination, meditation, communication, and astral travel. Any of these uses alone can be good reason to have a magic mirror handy, and all of them figured into our choice to include one as a cross-quarter tool on our altar. A small hand mirror is most practical in terms of size, and we prefer a standard mirror instead of a black scrying mirror because you can scry just as well with both types, but black mirrors can alter reflective meditation in ways that you may not always want.

It's a good idea to cleanse a mirror with salt or saltwater before consecrating it as a ritual tool, and washing a mirror with an infusion of mugwort can make it particularly good for scrying. Some people paint sigils on the backs of a mirrors to make sure that no one can secretly spy on them from the other side, while others place the scourge or a grounding stone on top of a magic mirror to ensure that it is "off" when not in use.

Like everything else on the altar, the mirror is both tool and symbol. Just as we feel it is important to see ourselves reflected on our athames, we also feel it is important to see ourselves reflected on our altar. One of our primary reasons for creating an inclusive and expanded ritual system was to represent diverse identities. Literally seeing ourselves on our altar symbolizes how our work represents who we are, and that is both a celebration of what we created together, and a reminder that we show our true selves in what we do and how we do it.

Deity Symbols

For each deity we call upon in circle, we place a small symbol on the altar in addition to Their candle. These symbols can be a stone or an herb favored by that deity; a small statue, figurine, or picture of that deity; or any other object that would be pleasing to or otherwise appropriate for Them. For example, a piece of deer antler would be a good choice for Artemis, a small hammer would work for Thor, or a model horse would be appropriate for Epona.

The deity symbols on our altar call the names of the Gods in ritual language. They are the physical, tangible counterpart to the titles and epithets we speak when we address Them, providing a multisensory element to our petition. Most deities are beautifully complex, and in ritual we often focus on specific parts of Their personality or domain. The symbols we use help specify which aspect of the deity we want to reach out to. Calling out to Artemis with a piece of deer antler will produce a very different effect from calling out to Her with a bloody arrowhead, or with a child's toy. All of them are perfectly appropriate symbols, but each calls upon very different parts of Her.

The more effort we put into selecting deity symbols, the more compelling our petition will be. If you're not sure what symbol to use for the deity you plan to approach in ritual, do some research and find out what They will like. That preparatory work of learning about the deity, Their preference, and Their customs is not only necessary for respectful ritual, it will also make your ritual generally more productive and effective.

Human Symbols

The larger a coven gets, the harder it is for everyone to attend every circle. Rather than capping their membership number, some groups handle this with member symbols. Each coven member selects a small object that resonates with them in some way. They privately consecrate this item, charging it with their energy and connecting it to their presence, perhaps by wearing it on their person for a few days, or by sleeping with it at night. The group leader keeps all the members' symbols with the coven's ritual tools. Whenever a person is unable to physically attend circle, their symbols is placed upon the altar as a way of including their energy and welcoming their presence in spirit.

Similarly, some groups place symbols of ancestors or honored dead on the altar for the same purpose. The symbol can be a picture of the person, a ritual tool they used in life, an object that alludes to their personality, or anything else that helps establish a connection. These symbols should be used as invitations, not demands—we want our beloved dead to feel welcome in circle with us without trying to force them to attend.

The Broom

Sometimes the most obvious objects make the best magical tools. When we need to clean interfering energies from a space, the broom serves as a perfect focus for our intent. The obvious connection between mundane and magical use makes it easy for everyone present to add their energy to a ritual sweeping. In fact, the psychological association with brooms and the concept of being "swept clean" can make ritual sweeping cathartic for everyone who witnesses it rather than just the space that is swept.

The correspondences mentioned above for herbs and woods can be applied to broom making. Some traditions have special recipes for their brooms, specifying particular types of wood for the handle, certain plants for the bristles, and various herbs and stones to included when binding them together. If you decide to make your own broom, consider the following as you select your materials:

❖ The handle is the end you'll be holding as you sweep, so it should be made of wood with magical attributes appropriate for your group's energy or identity.

❖ The bristles can be made of thin branches from a tree, or sprigs of dried herbs.

❖ Some dried herbs easily crumble when you try to sweep with them; test a sprig or two before you dry a large amount to make sure that herb is a practical choice.

❖ Plants associated with purification and cleansing make the best choice for bristles.

❖ Bind the bristles to the shaft with a natural material; willow was the historical choice for both magical and mundane brooms, but twine made from jute, sisal, cotton, or hemp can work just as well.

It's worth noting that the broom, like the bell, has some traditionally heterosexual associations: the phallic shaft nestled in the bristles can be a symbol of penetrative sex. We chose to maintain this lore about the broom, even though we don't intentionally work with heterosexual energy every time we use one. Heterosexuality is, after all, a valid part of our spectrums of orientation and identity, and our goal with Spectrum Gate Mysteries was not to eliminate all traces of heterosexuality, but to create a system that equally supports all shades and hues of identity. The heterosexual connotations of the broom are worth maintaining for their potential use in various acts of magic—for example, someone wanting to conceive a child might leap over a broom as a fertility rite.

It's also worth noting that penetrative sex need not be exclusively heterosexual. A Queer approach to the broom could include using it as a tool for sympathetic sex magic with any combination of genders. This symbolism can even be enhanced by using plants with traditionally gendered energy. A shaft of birch in mugwort bristles could make an excellent broom for working with lesbian energy, or a shaft of oak in holly bristles could create powerful gay magic.

The Staff

The staff is a situational tool, an object we use only when necessary for the particular ritual we have planned. We like to have a staff handy whenever possible because it is another effective grounding tool, but we don't consider it an essential feature of every circle. The staff is a defensive weapon, and its primary function for our group is just that: protection. It is wielded by the Guardian when we have need of one (for more on officiating roles, see page 55), and is used to protect our circle from outside interference. Generally speaking the interference we're concerned about is energetic, as the occasions when we feel we need a Guardian are when we're performing private ritual in a public space like a park or wildlife reservation. The Guardian can use the energy within the staff to ward off curious spirits, or divert errant currents

Have you been appointed to aid in diverting those who are uneducated or unaware of what your group is doing? Some useful phrases for diverting strangers include:

"We're having a private social gathering. Please give us space."

"We're rehearsing a performance. Please don't interrupt."

Consider having your Guardian carry a recording device and pretend to use it. People passing by often assume the ritual is some kind of entertainment production, and keep walking without asking any questions at all. At the same time, the Guardian should be wary of onlookers pulling out phones or tablets, as they might be photographing or recording your ritual without consent.

of energy that might interfere with our work. If a stranger happens to wander by, the Guardian would politely ensure that they do not intervene.

Part of what makes the staff an effective tool for defensive magic is that it is an actual weapon. Our group uses a bo staff as our ritual tool, scratched and dented from years of practice in its use. Whatever you choose to use as your ritual staff will be more effective in its magic if it could actually be used for combat should the need arise. That said, we do not recommend needless violent conflicts with passersby. Body language is often enough to express a desire for privacy, and when that fails polite conversation is often effective.

If words are ineffective, know your legal rights in the area where you gather, and proceed appropriately according to the law. Using public space for your ritual is a choice, and choosing to do so means accepting the rules and customs that go with that place. Of course, if you find yourselves physically assaulted, then by all means protect yourself. We are not defenseless. We wish to coexist peacefully, but we will take care of ourselves when we must.

The Sword

While it is a generally powerful tool, the sword is situationally useful. Some traditions consider the sword a symbol of the coven, and thus only those of sufficient rank to run their own coven are permitted to own a ritual sword. In SGM we are less concerned with the technicalities of rank, but agree that the sword should be kept by whoever leads the coven.

Like the athame, the sword is made of double-edged steel, and as such is associated with unbiased thought and discernment. While the athame is an individual tool, with each initiate possessing their own, the sword is a group tool, each coven having only one, again, typically owned or at least ceremonially kept by the leader of the group. In fact, passing the coven sword from one person to another is a traditional way of ritually observing a shift in coven leadership.

Because of the sword's relevance to the whole group, the unbiased thought and discernment of the sword takes on a more communal flavor, making the sword a tool of justice. We use the sword in circle when oaths must be sworn, the swearer speaking their oath with their hands upon the blade of the sword as a sign that they will accept the justice brought to them by their coven and by the Gods should they break their word.

Of course, the sword too is a weapon, and as a magical tool it functions best if it would be effective for its mundane purpose; ornamental swords just don't pack the same punch as a fully functional blade. In circles where protective magic is particularly important, we use the sword in place of the athame to bolster our defenses.

The author's sword, custom forged by a local smith, resting on a wood and leather sheath hand-crafted by a local Pagan Transwoman.

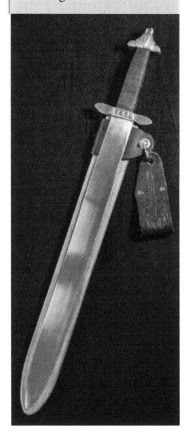

Setting An Altar

A properly set altar is can be considered another magical tool in and of itself. When every item is placed upon it in a way that compliments the whole and works towards your purpose, the result is a platform of power that significantly enhances your ritual. Consequently, for groups consisting of only two members, the altar can serve as the Anchor for your circle (for more on officiating roles see page 55).

There is no single correct way to set an altar. As with our selection of ritual tools, we have a default orientation and layout that we practice (see page 23), but sometimes the default doesn't work, and items must shift relative to one another and relative to the space you're in.

Traditionally each of the four elements is associated with a cardinal direction, so ritual tools associated with that element would be placed on that quadrant of the altar. We found those directional associations to be problematic because they not only determined altar placement for various tools, but also determined where certain ritual actions took place, most notably calling the elemental quarters. Sometimes that seemed to work well enough, as there is a certain power calling quarters in the same direction that so many others call them, but at other times it was just silly. For example, it makes absolutely no sense while casting a circle on an east coast beach to turn your back to the ocean and face west while calling upon elemental water.

We needed a system that did not depend entirely on traditional associations, but rather allowed officiators to position the altar, our tools, and the elemental quarters in locations that make sense for the landscape we are on at any given moment. Since that landscape will not be the same for every circle, our system needed to be adaptable and modular. It made sense to have a default setting to use when there is no compelling reason to do otherwise, as we've already discussed the values of prescribed ritual as a common spiritual language, but our default is made to be modified.

An altar set for a Beltaine ritual. One chalice holds an alcoholic beverage, and the other a non-alcoholic beverage. Food offerings include wheat toast with honey and gluten-free pasta with butter.

Shape

We use a round altar placed in the center of our circle. On a purely geometric level, the circle reminds us of a spectrum, with its single curve and lack of points or lines. We can also contemplate concentric circles in the altar as a reflection of the circle, and the circle as a reflection of our world.

On a more practical level, it is easy for a group to gather about a round altar without anyone being pushed farther out or drawn farther in than anyone else. It also allows us to work with any number of officiators and orient them around the altar in any position we wish in order to work with specific dynamics between and among them. It's certainly possible to do this with an altar of any shape simply by positioning people accordingly regardless of the shape of the altar, so if you don't have a round table to use, feel free to go with what you've got, making your people and your tools fit as best they can. Nevertheless, having a physically round altar lends a symmetry and flow to everything that we find not only appealing, but useful and effective.

There's no need to go out and buy special ritual furniture. Coffee tables and end tables make excellent altars, so you can use what you already have, or refinish a table that no one wants anymore. You could also repurpose an industrial spool; some hardware stores will give away wooden spools after they've sold the wire or cable they carried.

Size

The size of your altar is an entirely practical matter. It should be small enough for your group to gather around comfortably without feeling that they are too far away from it or one another, yet large enough to fit all of your ritual tools. Larger groups usually work better with a larger altar, and smaller groups often function well with one just big enough to fit all the tools. although sometimes that fit is pretty snug!

Keep in mind that at various times you will want to include objects beside your typical ritual tools on your altar for use in specific celebrations or magical workings. Consider using an altar with enough space for a few extra items, even if you have a smaller group.

Orientation

The "orientation" of a round altar means determining where each elemental quarter will be located, as ritual tools are arrayed on the altar according to their quarter or cross-quarter associations. These elemental quarters should correspond with the natural features of the land around you. Is there a mountain or forest nearby? That would be a solid choice for your earth quarter. Are you next to a lake, stream, or beach? That's an obvious place for the water quarter. Is there a breathtaking vista in one direction, or a place from which the wind blows more strongly? That's a good spot for air. Is there a kitchen or firepit nearby? That could be a good choice for fire. If only one or two natural features stand out strongly, then place the quarters that do speak to you where they need to be, and fill in the others where they make the most sense.

Our default order for elements going clockwise around the circle is fire, air, water, and earth. We chose to arrange the elements from least dense to most dense, with earth leading back to fire because it can combust a solid, starting the cycle of ignition to manifestation once again. In urban and suburban areas, we've often found that only a single natural feature strongly inspires us regarding the placement of an elemental quarter. Sometimes that inspiration differs even in a place where we circle frequently, depending on what type of magic or ritual we plan to do, which elements we want to emphasize in that work, and which dynamics we want to employ.

For more information on the elements, how they relate to the natural world, and how they influence magic and ritual, take a look at Scott Cunningham's *Earth Power: Techniques of Natural Magic* (1983), and *Earth, Air, Fire, and Water: More Techniques of Natural Magic* (1991). The better acquainted you become with the elements and their energy, the easier it will be for you to figure out how you want to include them in your ritual.

Layout

The Anchor (see page 56) is the officiator responsible for setting the altar because their job is to keep all of us rooted in our work, and the altar is the physical symbol for that work. Sometimes the Anchor embraces this task as a form of meditation in preparation for their role in circle, while at other times it is appropriate or even necessary for them to enlist the help of others. However, even when the Anchor delegates part or all or altar setup, it is still their responsibility to make sure the job gets done.

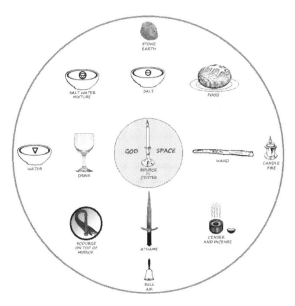

In Spectrum Gate Mysteries, the dominant hand is associated with will, and the non-dominant hand with discipline. When we reach out naturally for what we want, it is usually with our dominant hand, while reaching out with our non-dominant hand is typically a small exercise in self-control. When setting or moving tools upon the altar, one should use their dominant hand, because it is an act of will and conscious intent to set the altar as we do.

In the very center of the altar we place the source candle, the symbol of immense immanent divinity and the interconnectedness of all that is. The area immediately surrounding the source candle—the innermost ring on the altar—is what we call "God Space". Within this ring we orient the candles and symbols of the deities we plan to work with in circle. We place these with attention paid to the natures, preferences, and dynamics of the deities as they relate to the elements, our intent, and each other.

The next closest ring to the source candle is where we place our elemental tools. The wand is our tool of fire, and rests with the tip pointing in toward the source candle in the center, and the grip pointing out towards the fire quarter. The Builder's athame rests on the altar as the tool of air, with the blade pointing in towards the source candle, and the hilt pointing out towards the air quarter. The cup is the tool of water, resting in the water quarter, and the salt goes in the earth quarter as the tool of earth.

The furthest ring from the source candle is where we place the representatives of each element: a candle in the fire quarter, the bell in the air quarter, freshwater in the water quarter, and a stone in the earth quarter. This system of using concentric rings for the elemental items creates an altar that moves from the most inarticulable and metaphorical—the source candle in the center—to the most literal and physical—the elements themselves.

Between each quarter we place our cross-quarter tools: the incense, the mirror with the scourge placed atop it, the salt water mixture, and the food with the libation bowl stored beneath. We place these according to however they best fit within the orientation of our quarters. In the default orientation, incense goes between fire and air because it burns and creates fragrant smoke, the mirror and scourge go between air and water because both reflection and the wisdom of suffering combine thought with emotional awareness, saltwater goes between water and earth because it is a literal combination of the two, and food goes between earth and fire both because it is a substance often cooked and because it provides energy to our physical bodies.

We place the scourge on top of the mirror to represent the discipline and difficulty of honest introspection. It is a hard thing to look at oneself critically yet fairly, to assess where we are strong and where we are weak, and take steps to become more authentic to who we are and who we want to be. It is too easy to look at ourselves with vanity, seeing only what we like, or with unbalanced criticism, seeing only the worst of what we are. The scourge atop the mirror reminds us to expend the necessary effort to balance our introspection.

The cleansing, consecration, and mixing of salt and freshwater to create a saltwater mixture is part of the altar setting duties to be performed by the Anchor. (For a description of how this is done, refer back to page 33.

The broom, staff, and sword are not normally placed upon the altar. The broom rests at the outer edge of the circle in the quarter where circle casting will begin and end. We determine this quarter by designating a dominant element—the element most relevant to the magic, celebration, or ritual we have planned. When there is no obvious choice for a dominant element because multiple (or even all) elements are relevant to our work, we choose a dominant element based on what emphasis we want to add to our ritual. For example, we'd choose fire for passion and energy, air for wisdom and mental insight, water for intuition and empathy, and earth for physical manifestation and concrete success.

The staff and the Guardian go together: when one is needed in circle, so is the other. The staff is not placed on the altar because it is constantly in the hands of the Guardian. Either the Guardian will be using the staff to protect the circle, energetically if not physically, or the Guardian will hold the staff steady and vertical with its base planted on the ground while members grasp it for grounding—excess energy flows from the person into the staff, and the Guardian directs it down into the Earth.

The sword is almost always worn in a belted sheath, either by the Builder or by the group leader. One possible exception is when the sword is being used in place of the Builder's athame to enhance the defensive capacity of the circle. In such a situation, the sword could be placed on the altar as the tool of air to emphasize its role in protecting the circle. Another exception could be when the coven plans to work magic around the group itself, and wants the sword upon the altar as a symbol of the coven.

The Greeter should wear their athame in such a way that it is easily accessible when it is necessary in circle—typically in a sheath that hangs from a cord or belt. Their blade is not used a tool or symbol on the altar, but they will need it to cast the circle.

Ideally the altar will have enough food and drink on it for everyone to partake during ritual, plus enough for the initial food blessing described on page 39. However, sometimes very large groups will need to refill their cup while they pass it around the circle, as it should not be allowed to run empty until the toast. Consequently, it is wise to keep some extra drink stocked beneath the altar just in case more is necessary. The food for circle should be measured out beforehand, such that there is enough for everyone to have a share, plus a portion for each of the deities you call upon. If your plate or altar can't accommodate that much food, store a little extra under the altar next to the drink.

Once the altar is set and the participants are ready to start, the Anchor pauses to thank the spirits of the land. This need not be overly elaborate, but we feel it is important to offer gratitude to the spirits of place wherever you are, and to promise them that—excepting rituals in which pre-negotiated land magic or healing is the entire point—their home will be left just as you found it when you're done.

With this final step complete, the Anchor lights the Source candle as a signal that circle is about to begin, and all participants should turn their attention to the purpose of the ritual. The Anchor then lights the other altar candles from the source candle, and the incense or incense charcoal from the fire candle.

Casting A Circle

Now that you've got everything set up and have a basic idea of what it's all for, how do you put all that together to make a ritual? The first step in understanding how we cast a Spectrum Gate Mysteries circle is understanding how we determine who does what.

Officiating Roles

Until now, we have merely hinted at some of our officiators and their roles in casting a circle. It's time to dig a little deeper and learn more about what we chose and why.

As I mentioned above, we intentionally chose not to use terms like "priest" and "priestess" for our officiating roles because we wanted anyone of any gender to be able to take on any role and bring the unfiltered energy of their identity into their work. This meant looking at the essential components of circle casting and dividing the work in a way that made sense relative to function, not gender. We also wanted our officiating roles to be mutable and adaptable, just like the rest of our system. Consequently, while we operate with a default of three officiators—the Builder, the Anchor, and the Greeter—we allow for a minimum of two, and a maximum of however many roles you can think up and fit in your ritual.

Our minimum is two because the entire point of coven craft is to work in a group. If someone is performing ritual by themselves, they should do whatever they want or need to satisfy their own spirituality. When a group of two get together for an SGM circle, one should act as the Builder, while the other acts as the Greeter, and the altar fills in for the Anchor.

The Builder is responsible for creating the metaphysical constructs of energy that both make up, modify, and exist within the circle itself. They are the energetic heavy-lifters, and as such will benefit from an ability to sense, direct, and manipulate energy.

The Greeter is responsible for calling out to deities and spirits during ritual, as well as performing other recitations of liturgy or improvised verse. They are the ambassador of the circle, and as such will benefit from a knack for public speaking or ritual drama.

The Anchor is responsible for keeping the energy of the officiators and the participants firmly rooted in the task at hand. They are the tether that stabilizes the circle, and as such will benefit from an ability to keep themselves and the people around them focused and grounded.

As described on page 45, when circling outdoors in a public space, we like to have a Guardian whose job it is to stand at the edge of the circle and ensure that nothing interferes with our work. If the area is reasonably secluded, the Guardian can join us in the circle and participate in the ritual, but their primary focus must always be on the boundaries of the space so that they are ready to intervene at a moment's notice. In particularly busy areas, whether the traffic is physical or spiritual, the Guardian should remain on the edge of the circle, fully focused on guarding our space. Consequently the Guardian must be someone who appreciates the importance of their role, and is both willing and able to step out when needed without feeling left behind.

For particularly elaborate rituals it can be very helpful to have an Assistant whose job it is to help the other officiators with whatever tasks need doing. This can be as simple as fetching supplies during setup, or as complex as providing aftercare for an officiator or participant following a particularly challenging rite. Because the Assistant's job varies so widely depending on what is needed, it is important to discuss beforehand exactly what those needs are and how to meet them. Only then will you be able to assess who is best suited to fill that role. Sometimes multiple Assistants are necessary, either because aftercare will be required for more than one person, or because the help needed is diverse enough that no single person has every necessary skill. It's perfectly reasonable to have more than one Assistant; just make sure you determine beforehand who is responsible for what.

Your group can create as many officiating roles as you feel are necessary for each circle you perform. If you're planning a ritual that involves scourging, and one of your members has particular skill with the tool, perhaps they could be the ritual Scourger. If your ritual will include scrying and you have a member with a natural talent for the mirror, consider letting them be the ritual Diviner. Some groups like to have an officiator for each element, each one being responsible for the appeals to their quarter.

Remember that officiating roles can change from circle to circle (coven roles, however, are a bit different—see page 148), so if your group tries an officiating role that doesn't work for any reason, you can always do things differently next time. As your group gets started, there will be a normal period of experimentation in which you learn what works for you by trying things in different ways. Make time to check in with each other between rituals and talk about how things went and how you want them to go in the future.

Circle Casting Outline

The following is an easy-reference outline for casting a circle in Spectrum Gate Mysteries. Each step is listed along with the officiator(s) responsible for it:

- ❖ **Call to Presence:** *Greeter*
- ❖ **Sweeping:** *Anchor*
- ❖ **Casting:** *Anchor, Builder, and Greeter*
- ❖ **Censing:** *Greeter*
- ❖ **Asperging:** *Builder*
- ❖ **Calling Quarters:** *Anchor, Builder, and Greeter*
- ❖ **Petitioning Deities or Spirits:** *Greeter*
- ❖ **Statement of Intent:** *Greeter*
- ❖ **Sacred Work:** *All Participants*
- ❖ **Food and Drink:** *Anchor, Builder, and Greeter*
- ❖ **Thanking Deities or Spirits:** *Greeter*
- ❖ **Dismissing Quarters:** *Anchor, Builder, and Greeter*
- ❖ **Dispersing:** *Builder*
- ❖ **Closing:** *Greeter*

The Call To Presence

We begin our circle with what we describe as a call to presence: the Greeter performs some action with the intent of drawing everyone's attention to the present moment, helping them become fully mentally, physically, and spiritually engaged in the ritual we're about to perform. We want this engagement to be specific to what we're doing, so the call to presence changes depending on our intent. For a joyful celebration the Greeter might sing or play a song, inviting others to join in if they like. For a more somber affair, the Greeter might ring the bell once, letting the tone fade completely before proceeding, or ring it a specific number of times that is relevant to our ritual. To prepare for an act of magic, the Greeter might lead the group in breathing together, dynamically synchronizing our energy for the work ahead.

At least some of our rituals will involve themes of community and group identity. As such, it can be helpful to have a default call to presence, something everyone in your group instantly recognizes. Sometimes this organically becomes whatever call to presence you happen to use in your first circle. Other times it is the call to presence you happen to use most often, which naturally becomes a group favorite. Some groups intentionally choose a call to presence for their coven. Some traditions have a default call to presence that becomes a sort of hallmark of that particular denomination of the Craft. In any case, the benefit of the default is that it creates another point of commonality between members, and when participants hear it at the beginning of a circle, it immediately intensifies their sense of community. When you hear a familiar call to presence at the start of circle, you feel at home, and know that you belong.

Sweeping

The Anchor helps us maintain a connection to the corporeal reality of our work, so it is their job to sweep our ritual space. The broom presents a powerful union of physical and magical function. The Anchor sweeps dirt and dust off the floor, but also sweeps out any stagnant energies cluttering our space or our participants.

We have the anchor sweep clockwise around the circle three times, moving the bristles in tiny counterclockwise circles as they go. In the northern hemisphere, clockwise circles echo the movement of the sun around the earth, and so are associated with creating and moving forward. Balancing this, counterclockwise circles are associated with dispersing and deconstructing. The Anchor makes the first circuit around the circle when they sweep, and we wanted this circuit to be clockwise, setting a tone of production and progress for our work, but since the entire point of sweeping is to get rid of interfering energies, we move the bristles counterclockwise. If you live in the southern hemisphere, this should be reversed.

Sometimes the Greeter will sing a song or speak while the Anchor sweeps, the words being either something that is relevant to the act of sweeping, or an explanation for guests. In a private circle with only core coven members in attendance, and particularly when the occasion is somber, the group can focus silently on the Anchor's work, concentrating on letting their own stress and mental static to be swept away as well.

Casting

In Coven Craft the term "casting" can refer both to the entire process of creating a circle—from the call to presence to either the statement of intent or the final closing—and to the specific act of creating the energetic sphere that marks, wards, and contains sacred space. The most active officiator in the casting phase of creating a circle is the Builder, but both the Anchor and the Greeter assist them.

The Greeter participates in casting by speaking or singing a rhyme, verse, or song that focuses participants' attention and energy on the act of creating the magic sphere. The Anchor gathers this energy, maintains a steady ground for balance, and sends the group's assembled power to the Builder. The Builder shapes the energy into a great sphere that encompasses the altar, all the participants, and whatever extra space is needed. When circling indoors, the Builder often pushes this energy container to the edges of the room we are in, so that the physical walls and magical walls coincide.

Depending on the type of ritual we have planned, the Builder uses either the athame or the wand to direct energy and form the circle. The athame produces a stronger defense, and tends to pull us farther from mundane reality, putting us deeper into the realm of spirit. The wand creates a gentler container, better for celebrations and circles with guests. Selecting an appropriate wood for the wand can also add specific flavors to the energy of the space.

Casting begins with the Builder holding their tool of choice in the quarter of the dominant element, pointing it out toward the edge of the space they plan to designate. They then proceed along the edge of the circle moving clockwise, shaping the energy as they go. They complete three circuits, making sure that the circle is free of holes and reinforced as necessary, and end in the same place they began. Once again, clockwise motion for this and any other trips around the circle is specific to the northern hemisphere, and should be reversed in the southern hemisphere.

The particular type of energy the Builder uses, the metaphysical composition of the sphere itself, is a difficult thing to describe. Like a color someone's never seen before, or a flavor they've never tasted, it is clear once experienced, but until then the best we can do is describe it from context. The Builder's goal in wielding this energy is to create a protected space that is between the physical world and the spiritual world, and as such half in and half out of the flow of time (and for this reason we suggest that participants not wear watches in circle).

Neopagans tend to view reality as consisting of multiple planes or dimensions. One useful way of looking at these planes is to divide them into physical, mental, and spiritual. The physical plane is where our bodies exist and operate, the mental plane is where our ideas, archetypes, and preconceptions exist, and the spiritual plane is where Gods and spirits exist. This is certainly not the only way of conceptualizing elements of reality, but, for our purposes, the point is that the circle both exists between and touches all of them.

Most people tend to focus on the physical plane most of the time, and for good reason. We must be able to operate efficiently in a physical world in order to pay the bills, and many of life's joys and wonders are corporeal experiences, from the sensual pleasures of making love to the breathtaking awe of viewing a gorgeous natural landscape. Furthermore, living your daily life too far invested in any of the other planes can come with some serious drawbacks: immersing yourself in the mental plane leads to existing in a world where everything you think is true *is* true, and you fall out of touch with physical reality; immersing yourself in the spiritual plane can lead to an intimate relationship with Those who live there, but comes at a price of mental and physical health.

In a properly cast circle, participants act in all planes at once, and do so in a way that preserves their mental, emotional, physical, and spiritual health. The circle is between planes and in all planes, within time and outside time. We achieve that state partly by virtue of the whole circle-casting technique, from setting the altar to closing the ritual, and partly by the nature of the energy we use to craft the ward that surrounds us. Casting a circle is not just a ritual; it is a journey.

Censing

With the energetic walls of the circle ready to be blessed and sealed, the Greeter carries the censer once around the circle, consecrating the space with incense smoke, beginning and ending in the quarter of the dominant element. As they go, they speak our intent in sanctifying the circle, declaring it hospitable for Those we intend to approach. We assigned this duty to the Greeter because it readies our circle, its contents, and its participants for communion with the divine; thus we regard it as an ambassadorial act of preparation.

Typically the Greeter pauses in each quarter, taking a moment to think of each of the elemental guardians and prepare a space specifically for them. Sometimes the Greeter also pauses before each participant, wafting smoke over them to prepare them for what's ahead. Either way, the end result is that the circle is made ready for divine presence.

Asperging

In a final act of preparation and construction before we call upon other entities in our sacred space, the Builder carries the salt water once around the circle, beginning and ending in the quarter of the dominant element. As they go, they sprinkle salt water on the space, the participants, and even the altar, either using their fingers to flick little droplets, or using a sprig from an appropriate plant as an aspergillum. Sometimes the Greeter or even the Builder themselves will speak about purification and solidity as the Builder asperges, but often we let this last act pass in silence, contemplating the sacred work we are about to carry out.

We cense our circle before we asperge it for a few reasons. For one, we like how this spreads the elements around our circle in our preferred order: fire and air in the smoke, then water and salt in the mixture. We also appreciate asperging as a reference to washing, the final act performed before imploring the Gods in many forms of ancient ritual. Most important, however, is that we use salt water as a fixative. All the magic of creating and consecrating the circle is sealed into place with salt water. We prefer saltwater over salt for this purpose because it is stable yet fluid, and combines physical manifestation with intuition. It is for this reason that we assign the job of asperging to the Builder; they are responsible for the metaphysical construction of our circle, so they should be the one to seal it in place.

Calling Quarters

Now that the sphere of the circle is in place, the next step is to invite elemental allies to join our circle. The Greeter is responsible for speaking formal invitations to each element. Because the space has been warded against intruders, as each element is called, the Builder must create a gateway by which those spirits can enter the circle. Once again, the Builder is assisted in this by the Anchor, who stabilizes the energies of the other participants so that the Builder can better utilize it.

Some Pagans treat the elements as vast powers that are unpersonified. When they call Fire to circle, for example, they call on the elemental power of combustion and heat, and welcome that energy into their sacred space. This is particularly common in non-traditional Neopaganism, and is useful for groups that tend to be less theistic, or who don't believe in elemental spirits. This can be somewhat problematic for our purposes, however, as part of the point of employing elemental spirits in circle is to ask for their protection. Having placed ourselves in a vulnerable position between worlds, and wanting to focus on whatever work we have planned for our ritual, we need someone or something to watch our backs. This is the traditional role of the elemental spirits called into circle, sometimes referred to as guardians or "watchtowers". While working with elemental energy instead of spirits can be effective in circle, groups that do this should consider alternate methods of bolstering their defenses. For light-hearted seasonal celebrations such measures may not be necessary, but strong protection is necessary for the vulnerability of intense spiritual work.

Elemental spirits don't always show up just because you call. The process of encountering the elements and developing a relationship with each is a part of Craft training that can't be delivered through a book. In an existing group this is not a problem, as established members call upon the guardians they already know while new members create their own connections. If you're looking to start your own group, however, doing some of this work before your first circle is a good idea.

Perhaps thanks to the frequency with which Neopagans call upon them, the elemental spirits seem to be accustomed to people asking for their protection. Fitting into that well-worn magical grove is not terribly difficult, but humility and gratitude go a long way. A respectful approach to establishing a relationship with elemental spirits means physically going to a place where that element is prominent, mentally focusing on its attributes, and emotionally and spiritually opening yourself to communing with it. Speak your intent, and be thankful for whatever response you get.

Calling upon the protection of elemental spirits is often referred to as calling quarters because each element is asked to grant protection for its quarter of the circle. To call each element, the Greeter stands in that element's quarter facing outward, while the Builder stands behind them across the altar, also facing that quarter, and holding the bell in their hand. The Greeter holds out their athame, pointing it up towards the quarter in a sign of respect—we bear our weapons openly as a sign of good faith, a promise that we are not concealing our true intent, but also to remind any onlookers that we are not defenseless on our own. The Greeter calls out to the elemental spirit or spirits they are inviting, either by name or by title (e.g. "Guardian of Air"), after which the Builder rings the bell once, using its sound to create a gateway in the energetic sphere of the circle by which that specific spirit can enter. The Greeter then speaks a formal invitation to that spirit, requesting its protection and often also its aid in whatever ritual is planned. This invitation traditionally ends with "Hail, and welcome," which is repeated by the whole group. We also like to salute each quarter before we move to the next, and by salute we do not mean the military gesture, but a kiss. Each person kisses either their athame if they have one or the fingers of their dominant hand if they don't, and then points again out towards the element, sending that signal of respect to them.

Part of the utility of the salute is that it helps complete the circle. The quarter calls begin with the dominant element and then proceed clockwise around the circle. When all four elements have been called, the Greeter then returns to the quarter of the dominant element, and there the group performs one more salute, this time pointing both hands up in an open posture, saluting the entirety of the magic circle and assembled guardians, as well as the concepts of completion and balance.

Petitioning Deities or Spirits

Many traditions call the deities or spirits they wish to work with into their circle, formally inviting Them and creating special gateways in or through which They should appear. We chose to go a different route. For one, we figure that the Gods are powerful enough that if They want to be in our circle They will be, and if They don't, They won't, so the creation of fancy doors for Them is at the very least unnecessary, and perhaps a little insulting. To be fair, if you're working with a spirit rather than a deity, this might be different, but even then it depends on the nature of that spirit, and how you believe your circle functions in the context of what you're trying to do.

In SGM we believe that casting a circle is as much a journey as a ritual, and the place we're traveling to is where the Gods are. We don't call Them to us; we go to Them. Our petition is like ringing Their doorbell, and then explaining why we're here when They open the door. By default we have the Greeter perform this step, but when one of our participants has a personal connection to the deity we're approaching, we let them speak the petition instead if they prefer. The petitioner calls upon the deity by name and by as many epithets are appropriate, then describes why we've come and what we plan to do. The petitioner also explains why we are calling upon that deity in particular, whether it be for protection, assistance, or any other reason. Of course, since our circle is between spaces, when the

Gods let us into Their metaphorical house, we also let Them into ours. As a way of recognizing this shared space, and a way of letting everyone participate in the petition, the Greeter finishes with the traditional "Hail, and welcome," repeated by the whole group.

Statement of Intent

With the circle cast and all deities and spirits properly welcomed, the final step before beginning your celebration or magical working is to state your intent. Until now, the intent of the circle has been expressed in many ways, from the qualities called into the salt water mixture to the reasons given to each deity in the petitions. Now, however, is when the Greeter clearly and concisely states for all present why we came and what we plan to do. The statement of intent is a magical act, an expression of will that sets the course of the ritual. It is also a reminder that we cast circles only when there is need to do so. Whenever we journey to that sacred space, we must have a reason for being there.

The Greeter typically finishes with a phrase that is echoed by all participants so that the statement is a group effort, not just an act of the Greeter. Our favorite is the traditional "So mote it be" — "mote" in this context meaning something between "may", "must", "shall", and "required".

Sacred Work

With your circle cast and consecrated, now is the time to do what you came for. This should be the focus of your circle, where most of your energy is directed. In the section on Sacred Work (page 75), we will delve into different types of sacred work, exploring the various activities that work well in circle, and examining how to go about them effectively.

Food and Drink

The last act before beginning to disassemble the magic circle is sharing food and drink in a sacred meal. This serves both spiritual and practical purposes. Sharing food and drink is a well-established social mechanism for bonding. When we eat together, we become not just a group of people, but a community invested in supporting its members. By including the Gods in our meal, we strengthen our bonds not just with each other, but with Them as well. On a more practical level, eating and drinking help us return our attention to our physical bodies. Eating in particular tends to be naturally grounding (unless you're specifically eating something with a different effect). Consuming a little food in circle helps people come down from the energetic high of your ritual enough to focus on dismantling the circle and making a transition back to a primary focus on physical reality. For this reason the food and drink we share is not a full meal, but just enough to bring us back to our bodies and connect us to each other, while still being able to finish our ritual.

In a Traditional Wiccan circle, this sharing of food and drink often begins with what is called "the symbolic Great Rite," in which the tip of the athame is inserted into the cup, a symbol of a penis entering a vagina in heterosexual sex, blessing the drink with the power of sex, procreation, and binary polarity. We tried to make this work for Spectrum Gate Mysteries, creating a gender-neutral liturgy to go along with the athame-in-cup blessing, allowing anyone to hold either the cup or the athame, providing access to that procreative polar energy. While we came up with a functional option, we felt its utility was too narrow to keep as our default. We use it when we specifically want to work with polarity between two opposites as a source of power, but needed something different for our everyday food and drink blessing.

We found our answer through examining the meaning of the ritual tools used in the sacred meal: the cup and drink as a symbol of spiritual nourishment, the food as a symbol of social and physical nourishment, and the libation bowl as a symbol of sacrifice and our willingness to work for what we want. These three tools became the foundation for our new food and drink blessing.

The roles of the Anchor and Builder in the food and drink blessing vary depending on the intent of our ritual. For circles with a more human or community-based focus, the Anchor holds the food, rooting our nourishment in the physical nourishment we offer one another. For circles with a more divine or spirit-based focus, the Anchor holds the cup (or the pitcher, if you plan on pouring the drink into individual cups), rooting our magic in shared spiritual experience. The Greeter always holds the libation bowl, reaffirming our relationship of give-and-take with each other, and with the Gods.

Each holding their respective tool, the Anchor, Builder, and Greeter speak the following words to bless the food and drink. Because the roles change depending on the situation, our liturgy is scripted according to who is holding which tool.

Food: *We, the community*
Drink: *and the Gods we honor*
Libation: *and the path we walk*
All: *come together for a common goal*
Food: *in fellowship*
Drink: *and faith*
Libation: *and sacrifice*
All: *to become the future of our design*
Food: *of free expression*
Drink: *sincere connection*
Libation: *and fruitful exchange.*

As the final words are spoken, the officiators holding the food and drink each place a bit of their substance into the libation bowl:

All: *As we unite our efforts,*
we ignite the spark of creation,
and our work is done,
and our work begins.

This first act of offering is what blesses and consecrates our food. Once it is complete, food and drink are passed clockwise around the circle to be shared by all participants. Usually we do this casually and informally, as we appreciate the connective intimacy of passing food and drink like a family, and holding the libation bowl for one another. That said, if you have an Assistant that needs a task, or if you want to create a more formal ritual, carrying food, drink, and the libation bowl around the circle could certainly become ceremonial roles.

The cup should never be empty until everyone has gotten some food and drink, and the Greeter is ready to toast the Gods. If there's any doubt as to whether or not you'll have enough drink, keep more stored beneath the altar just in case. The primary reason for not letting the cup run dry is its symbolism as the tool of water, described on p. 29, but there is also a more functional purpose. The drink stored beneath the altar is not consecrated as the drink in the cup or pitcher during the blessing. However, when you add more drink to the cup, the consecrated drink still in it shares its blessing with what you add to it, so there is no need for another consecration.

The toast is another expression of gratitude, this time specifically directed to the divine. It also serves a practical social function. The sacred meal is typically somewhat informal. People can relax and chat with each other while they eat and drink. It's the first time since the ritual began that their focus may wander, and this is usually a needed break. The toast signifies the end of that interlude. It brings everyone's attention back to the ritual, and gets the group ready to dismantle the circle.

When everyone has had enough to eat and drink, and just enough time to relax without getting completely off course, the Greeter raises the cup towards the center of the circle. This signals that the toast is about to happen, and the group quiets and focuses on what the Greeter is about to say. The toast begins with "For the gifts of..." and then the Greeter names three things for which they and likely the entire group are thankful. These can be as vague as concepts like "community" or "stability", as specific as important moments for your particular coven, or as concrete as objects your group is grateful to have. The Greeter finishes the toast with "...we give thanks to the Gods!" Typically the Greeter pauses before the final "to the Gods," as that last phrase is echoed by the group in the formula of a normal toast. Of course, if "Gods" doesn't work for you as a gender neutral equivalent for deities, try "to the divine" instead, or any other variation that suits your group. After making the toast, the Greeter drains the cup, making sure that none of the consecrated drink is wasted, then places the cup upside down on the altar.

If your group uses a pitcher and individual cups in ritual, make sure the officiator holding the drink for the blessing uses the pitcher, not their individual cup, so that all of the drink gets consecrated. Each person should keep a bit of beverage in their glass for the final toast, and everyone should drink together with the Greeter. The Greeter's cup should be the one placed on the altar as the tool of Water in the appropriate quarter. All other cups can rest on the altar wherever is most practical, keeping an eye out for overall balance.

Thanking Deities or Spirits

The same deities petitioned during the circle casting should be thanked during its closing. The Greeter (or whoever spoke the original petition, if it was not the Greeter) does this in a similar style to the petition, using the same names and epithets, and expressing genuine gratitude for Their presence and assistance in the ritual. Once again, the sentiment here is not that we are sending Them away, but rather that we are about to leave, so we thank Them for sharing space with us before we go. The Greeter ends with "Hail, and farewell," which is repeated by the whole group.

Dismissing Quarters

The quarters are dismissed in a similar fashion to how they were called. The Greeter begins with the quarter of the dominant element and proceeds around the circle clockwise (or counter-clockwise in the southern hemisphere). Some groups do this in the opposite direction, as the intent here is not to create sacred space but dismantle it, and counterclockwise motion in the northern hemisphere is the direction associated with dispersing (clockwise in the southern hemisphere). In SGM we want to ensure that each elemental has the same amount of time in circle, emphasizing equal treatment of each and balance among them, so we dismiss the quarters in the same order we call them.

The Anchor, Builder, and Greeter perform the same general energetic roles here as in the quarter calls, only instead of creating the doorways, the Builder closes and disperses them. The Greeter thanks each element using the same names or titles used in their call, finishing with a "Hail, and farewell," repeated by the group with the same salute.

Dispersing

The Builder disperses the energetic sphere of the circle, leaving the energy of the space as it was when ritual began. The very fact that properly dismantled circles leave little impression on the land where they happen is a point of utility for circle casting as a ritual format. A space energetically charged from frequent ritual can become difficult to use for mundane purposes, especially for energy-sensitive individuals, but you can cast a circle in your living room at every Sabbat and still comfortably use it for anything else on any other day. The entire process of thanking deities, dismissing quarters, and dispersing the sphere contributes to the circle's ability to leave no trace, but the dispersal can be the most technically challenging of these stages.

Beginning in the quarter of the dominant element, the Builder points their athame outward and uses it to disperse the energy of the circle. Even wand-cast circles are still dispersed with the athame because both the ferrous properties of the athame's blade, and the tool's capacity to cut, assist with dispersing energy. Usually going once around the circle is enough, but sometimes three circuits are necessary. As with the casting, the technical how-to is almost impossible to articulate, and is part of why face to face training and direct experience can never be wholly replaced by books.

Dispersing can be done either clockwise or counter-clockwise depending on your need. When we've worked magic in circle that we don't want to be completely undone, such as a spell we want to take effect over time, or an act of empowerment you want to grow within you, we disperse clockwise so that the circle is closed, but not wholly undone. When our work in circle involved purification, catharsis, or cutting ties in some way, we disperse counter-clockwise, emphasizing that what was removed in circle is thoroughly and completely gone.

The Greeter often contributes with a verse as they did in the casting, but this is less essential for the dispersal. The point here is not to add energy but to get rid of it, so the Anchor has nothing to gather or send, and the group needs only to stay out of the Builder's way. The Greeter's verse can help people focus on keeping their energy to themselves, as can having participants stand with their arms crossed over their chest in what is often referred to as the Osiris position.

Closing

The circle should end with a final communal act of closing to ensure that everyone leaves with a sense of it being "done". This not only facilitates transition back into mundane reality, but also helps participants let go of whatever they might need to leave behind, and allows any magic set in place to do its work. Just as metal and clay become fragile if overworked, magic too must be given just enough effort, not too little, and not too much.

The Neopagan closing based on traditional Wiccan liturgy is some variation of "Merry meet, merry part, and merry meet again." That works well enough, and its ubiquity in the greater Pagan community makes it useful to know if only so that you'll recognize it when you hear it. Usually everyone recites it together, so if you hear it in a public ritual and know the words, you'll be able to participate.

That said, we wanted other options for Spectrum Gate Mysteries. The traditional parting didn't quite fit our group identity, being too strongly associated with Traditional Wicca for at least one of our members. We tried out poetry excerpts, which may provide a useful solution for some groups, but they just didn't catch on in our coven. Ultimately we wrote our own parting:

In sacred space we came
In every hue and shade,
And now we travel forth
As magic we have made.

If you like our verse, feel free to use it. If not, look for poems, verses, song lyrics, or anything else that speaks to your group as an appropriate end to your ritual. You'll want to pick something short and easy to remember so that everyone in your group can learn it and recite it from memory. Think about how you and your group want to feel walking away from ritual, and find or write something that captures that sentiment.

Sacred Work

What Is Our Work?

Casting circle with a coven becomes a shared ritual language that deepens our connection to the other members of our group, and allows us to engage more openly with our sacred work ... but what exactly is that work? Once the circle is cast, what do we do inside it? In this section, we'll discuss four broad categories of work that can be done in a circle: honoring deities and spirits, celebrating holidays, working magic, and rites of passage.

Deities and Spirits

Circles can be an excellent space in which to interact with deities and spirits, and they can be useful for people with widely varied approaches to theology. Being a polytheist, much of what I have to teach about honoring deities and spirits comes with a heavily polytheistic bias, and is expressed in polytheistic language. I invite you to interpret what you read here in whatever way works for you.

There is no single philosophy or religious belief necessary for a meaningful experience in circle. Atheists who believe deities are complex Jungian archetypes can create powerfully transformative magic alongside strict polytheists. Duotheists, henotheists, polytheists, and monotheists can stand together in circle and support each other's work. The key to achieving this sort of harmony despite philosophical and theological differences is accepting that it is OK to be different.

No two individuals have exactly the same experience of life, so why would they have the same experience of the Gods? Divinity and spirituality are neither binary nor strictly objective. Just because someone's experience is different from yours doesn't mean either of you are wrong. We interpret, internalize, and intellectualize our experiences in ways that infuse them with our own personal language. Each experience we have becomes uniquely ours. It's *supposed* to be different.

One of the benefits of working in a coven is that your group can decide if a common theology is something you want to share. Maybe you *want* to work in a group composed entirely of duotheists. Maybe concepts of divinity make you uneasy, and you really only feel comfortable talking about deities as archetypes. Maybe you get tired of having to explain polytheistic concepts of divine agency over and over, and really just want to worship with a group people who already get it. All of these are valid choices. You and your coven can decide if or how much philosophy and theology should be shared amongst your members.

When we approach the Gods in our circles, we must be careful to do so respectfully, and that respect is not just for the Gods Themselves, but for Their worshipers as well. Some of the pantheons commonly encountered in modern Paganism come from long-dead cultures, and it's easy to look at these pantheons and argue that there's nothing wrong with worshiping old Gods in new ways. Devotional polytheists might complain about appropriation, but—and I say this as a devotional polytheist—we are constructing something new just as much as they are. It might feel like we reconstructionists are reviving long dead practices, or preserving bits of ancient cultures that never died, but this view vastly oversimplifies the many complexities of those ancient cultures. We live in a very different society, and no matter how faithfully we try to recreate ancient traditions, they are different because we are different. In my opinion, both *should* be different.

Honoring deities from contemporary cultures becomes a bit more complicated. The Lwa spirits of Voudoun, for example, have their own traditions that are still very much alive. If someone is genuinely called to honor Them, why not do so in Their own way? The same could be said for the Japanese Kami, or the Gods of Hinduism. If the opportunity exists to learn their traditions, but we choose to honor Them in circle instead because it's easier for us, or because learning Their ways would be too hard, that seems terribly disrespectful.

Think of it this way: how long would you stay friends with someone who always made you drive an hour and a half to their house to visit them, but always refused to go to your place when you offer the invitation? Perhaps an arrangement could be made to take turns with who goes where— maybe people who honor modern Gods in Their own traditions can also respectfully call them in circle thanks to the relationship they've developed elsewhere. Sometimes people don't have access to a God's native traditions, so the only means they have for worship is in circle. Would that God be more understanding in such a situation? Is there a point at which that person would need to find a way to learn those other traditions? Or can a genuine personal connection surpass the challenges of culture differences?

I have no concrete answers to any of these questions that ring true for every situation. I believe that it is important for us to think carefully about how we interact with the Gods and with Their cultures, but perhaps there are no true answers, and only a general sense of genuine respect and humility can guide us in our interactions with others - whether those others be divine or not. Even when we're working with ancient Gods from long-dead cultures, it behooves us to research who those Gods were to the people who worshiped Them in antiquity. The myths, epithets, and ancient rituals of a God help us understand who They were and who They are, even if They manifest differently in our modern world. There are some modern Pagans who insist that historical knowledge is unnecessary, but if someone were trying to get to know you, how would you feel if they refused to acknowledge anything that had happened in your life before that day? Certainly you are a different person than you were a year ago, or five years ago, but doesn't your past contribute to who you are? And aren't there some elements of *you* that persist in how you've expressed yourself throughout time? When we completely reject history and lore, we tell the Gods that we don't really care about Them, we only care about who They will be for us. I certainly wouldn't appreciate being treated that way, and I suspect They don't either.

There are so many different deities and spirits one might approach in circle that writing about each of them (or, rather, most of them, as I doubt a truly comprehensive listing is practical, let alone possible) would constitute a book in and of itself. If you're not sure where to start, read some mythology from a variety of sources, and pay attention to what inspires you, what challenges you, and what you find compelling or curious. These are often the trailheads that lead toward relationships we need.

As you research, keep in mind that resources can vary greatly in quality. Even primary sources—ancient texts written by people who were part of that ancient culture or worshipers of that deity—must be translated; some translations are excellent renditions of the original meaning, while other can be confusing or downright misleading. Find out who translated a source you're reading, and be aware of their credentials.

Secondary sources—texts written by later authors about something they did not witness or were not a part of—can be excellently insightful, downright false, or anything in between. Academia is a decent place to look for good-quality secondary sources, but the department of academia will greatly affect the scholarship and perspective on what you read. For example, the fields of religious studies, political studies, classical studies, and women's studies all have very different things to say about ancient Greek religion. There's nothing wrong with collecting more information—if you're not sure who you agree with, keep reading. Learn as much as you can and decide what seems most plausible to you.

Some cultures won't have many or even any written texts. The best way to learn about those Gods will be through archaeology, which likely means relying on secondary sources that discuss archaeological finds. If you can visit a museum to see some of the artifacts in person, or visit sites of ancient worship, I highly recommend doing so, but for many that is an unattainable luxury. Once again, look for secondary sources that carry weight within academia, as these are most likely to be based on fact and plausibility. While academic texts tend to be fairly expensive to purchase, they are also more often available at a local public or university library.

Even if the Gods you're interested in do have many myths, archaeology and ancient practice are still worth consideration. The ancient Greek Gods, for example, appear very differently in myth than They did in cult practice. Comparing the two gives us an excellent view into both what role mythology played in the lives of ancient Greek people, and into who and what the Gods were—and are—to Their worshipers.

Many primary and even secondary sources are now available online. Internet archives are providing translations and even original texts of ancient literature, and some academic texts can now be rented as e-books. Nevertheless, be cautious in your use of Internet research, and evaluate every page with as much discernment as you can muster. It can be extremely difficult to assess the quality of information on a website until you've gotten at least some footing in the subject yourself.

Finally, for all that I advocate researching the history of the Gods you want to worship, I do not believe it can replace action and devotion. We exist now, in our modern society, and our religious and spiritual practice must reflect who we are, adapting to be relevant for our world. Even in history the Gods and Their manifestations were not static, so why would They be now? Surely They did not freeze Themselves at some arbitrary moment when ancient gave way to modern. As growing, learning, and developing individuals, we are who we were, who we are, and who we will become, all in this moment ... and so are They. Learn who They were, discover who They are, and grow with Them into the future.

Holidays

People celebrate holidays for a wide variety of reasons. Some want to recognize the changing seasons in a way that helps them keep in tune with the Earth. Some want to commemorate historical events and recognize how the past affects our present and our future. Some just want an opportunity to gather with other people and celebrate anything in a way that fosters community. Each coven will need to determine its own attitude towards holidays, decide which holidays they want to observe, and how they want to celebrate them.

In Spectrum Gate Mysteries, we decided to retain the eight holidays or Sabbats of traditional Wicca: Samhain, Yule, Imbolc, Ostara, Beltane, Litha, Lammas, and Mabon. These eight holidays have become tremendously common in modern Paganism, such that they can no longer truly be regarded as exclusively Wiccan. We want to feel connected to the greater Pagan community, and part of how we maintain that connection is by celebrating the same holidays.

All that said, we quickly found that some of the traditional activities associated with the Sabbats carried concepts of binary gender that were problematic for our group. We decided that while it is important to know how the Sabbats have historically been observed, we wanted to create our own ways of celebrating the core themes of each holiday.

I should note that the dates presented here are relevant for the northern hemisphere, and my seasonal observations reflect a moderately high northern latitude. I write with this bias solely because it is where I live. The Craft thrives at many latitudes on both sides of the equator. Groups practicing in the southern hemisphere celebrate the Sabbats on dates appropriate for their seasons, shifting the cycle by six months but keeping it otherwise roughly intact. As you read through this chapter on how the Sabbats emerge from natural cycles, I encourage you to think about how seasons manifest in your area, and how you might modify your rituals to reflect your landscape.

Finally, Sabbat celebrations can include both ritual activities to be performed in circle, as well as other activities that take place outside of circle. Connecting ritual acts to mundane work helps us feel a bond between what we do in circle and our daily lives. Holiday celebrations in particular are excellent opportunities to make our spiritual work relevant to our everyday existence, and to spread our magic out into the world.

Samhain

Perhaps the most famous of the Pagan Sabbats is Samhain, also known as All Hallow's Eve, or Halloween. In the mythology of Traditional Wicca, Samhain is when the Goddess of Life descends to the underworld hoping to solve the mystery of death. There She meets the God of Death, who first challenges Her with an ordeal, then falls in love with Her and teaches Her "mysteries" and "magics" (Gardner, 1954). Together with Beltane—which falls on May 1st, opposite Samhain on the wheel of the year—Samhain is referred to as a "hinge". The "hinges" are considered to be turning points in the year, when the veil between life and death is at its thinnest, and the currents of life energy and death energy shift. At Beltane life flows into the world. At Samhain, it flows out.

Because of these seasonal dynamics, Samhain is an excellent time to honor deities of death, and to remember and celebrate our own ancestors and beloved dead. Working with the dead can run the emotional gamut from joyous and nostalgic to painfully lonely. Sometimes people need a jovial celebration of their deceased loved ones, and sometimes they need to express their sorrow.

Working with ancestors and the dead can be particularly challenging for Pagans, and especially Queer Pagans. Many of us have familial dead who disapproved of us in life, and sometimes that disapproval was expressed with open hostility. Why would someone invite to circle a person who repeatedly called them a faggot, disowned them from their family, refused to recognize their gender, or physically beat them? Why would someone intentionally reconnect with a toxic relationship?

For some, the answer is that they don't. Some people find it far healthier and more constructive to let those threads of interpersonal connection thin and wither and eventually disintegrate. In the meanwhile, they establish and build relationships with ancestors of spirit, such as historical figures they feel a special kinship with, or deceased members of a tradition, clan, or chosen family. They reach out to people who lived lives that resonate with their own beliefs and goals, hoping that their spirits might provide the guidance and insight that blood ancestors give to some others.

If you choose this route, it is important to remember that building a relationship with a dead person is very much like building a relationship with a living person. It takes time, effort, and mutual respect. Don't expect to simply show up at their metaphorical doorstep and instantly be treated like family. Get to know them, and let them get to know you. You might find that they are good for you in ways you never would have expected, or that the relationship is not as wonderful as you thought it would be.

Just because you call on someone doesn't mean they'll answer. They may not like you as much as you like them. They might be unable or unwilling to develop the relationship you're asking for. Some people choose to become part of the Beloved Dead, and continue to serve their family or community as an ancestor. Others choose to transform and move on to whatever exists beyond death. If you reach for a person who has died but wishes to move on, demanding an ancestral relationship with them regardless of their own wishes, you might just get nothing—no response, no sense of presence, no spooky dreams full of wisdom from beyond the veil. Just nothing. If you push too hard, however, and actually manage to attach yourself to the spirit of a dead person against their will, you might actually hinder their ability to move on, leaving them stuck and static in an unproductive death. Forcing a ritual on someone against their will, even if your intent is to heal or "elevate" their spirit, is a violation of consent. If you care enough to attempt to help them, you ought to care enough to respect them as well. Sometimes people—living and dead—do not want your help, and they must be left to proceed on their own path. As you develop connections with ancestors of spirit, make sure to offer quiet moments of listening. Give them the opportunity to consent, and if they don't consent, leave them be. Let them transform into whatever they must become.

Some people find that ancestor work can be a way to heal toxic relationships. Sometimes death can give new perspective to someone who was bigoted or dysfunctional in life. These dead will often be apologetic to those they treated cruelly while they were living, and grateful for an opportunity to heal old wounds. Sometimes they find that they need the forgiveness of those they harmed in life in order to move on in death. Some Pagans practice rituals called "elevating the dead" in which the spirits of those whose were abusers in life are pushed to recognize their mistakes and make amends. Through reflection, forgiveness, and learning, these dead become better individuals than they were in life. The hope is that this process of "elevating" them will end a cycle of abuse by making them a better person for their next life.

Working with toxic ancestors can be just as healing for the living as it can be for the dead. Repressed feelings of hurt can turn into hate for others and for ourselves. Old wounds fester, and can infect every part of our lives in a sort of spiritual sepsis. By intentionally approaching family members who were cruel to us in life and attempting to heal those relationships in death, we can begin to heal our own hearts. Sometimes our blood ancestors are more understanding and accepting once death has shifted their perspective, and they are as eager to change an unhealthy dynamic as you are. Sometimes a dead person is just as obnoxious in death as they were in life, and working with them is not about healing a sick connection, but instead about finding a way to free oneself from internalizing their hate.

None of us are perfect, and all of us make mistakes. Sometimes we are the one who was cruel to someone who died. Sometimes we realize later in life that we were terrible in ways we didn't understand until we grew and changed through our experiences. Sometimes we didn't recognize how a careless comment could impact the psyche of someone already struggling with mental illness. Working with the dead can be as much about treating their wounds as it can be about treating our own. An apology from an abuser trying to make amends can be powerfully healing, but some victims need their abusers to be simply gone, and never want to interact with them again in any capacity. This is just as true for the dead as it is for the living. Some will accept and appreciate your attempt to make things right. Others will utterly reject your advances, and the only way to achieve healing for either of you is to respect that rejection and leave them be. One consent violation cannot be healed with another; abuse cannot absolve abuse.

As you and your group begin to consider if or how you might celebrate Samhain, ask yourselves the following questions:

❖ Who are your dead? Are they your blood ancestors? Are they adopted ancestors? Are they ancestors of spirit?

❖ Why do you want to celebrate the dead? Does your group need a chance to remember them? Do you need to vent your grief? Do want to connect to people you never knew well in life? Do you want to send messages to people who have died? Do you want to ask them for advice?

Once you have a sense of who you want to work with and what you want to accomplish for or with them, think about what you can do in circle to create the experience you need. Some examples include:

❖ A coven with a member grieving the recent and unexpected loss of a family member assists them in writing a letter of farewell to their dead relative, which can be ritually burned to carry the message across the veil.

❖ A group of transpeople choose to honor Trans victims of hate crimes as ancestors of spirit, lighting candles for them and telling joyous stories about the people they were in order to help them find peace in death and transition smoothly to whatever lies beyond.

❖ A coven invites friends and family members to join them for a pot-luck dinner which features favorite foods of deceased loved ones as a way of remembering the people who have passed and inviting their presence to return for a visit.

❖ A group struggling with the loss of members of their tradition set up a shrine for the ancestors of their chosen family, including candles, pictures, objects, and food; together they sit before the shrine, share stories of their dead, and express their grief as a community.

Yule

The winter solstice is celebrated in a wide variety of ways by countless different cultures and traditions. In modern Paganism, it is often called Yule after the ancient Germanic midwinter festival. In the mythology of

Traditional Wicca, the Goddess gives birth to the God of Light at dawn, so many groups vigil throughout the night, singing songs and celebrating with each other to support the Lady while She is in labor. Many modern Pagans also observe a contest between the Oak King and the Holly King, the Oak King being a god of summer and the Holly King a god of winter. They battle at Yule and at Litha, the summer solstice; at Yule the Oak King wins the fight, and light overtakes the world, whereas at Litha the Holly King wins, and the days grow steadily darker. Many Wiccans also create a special fire at Yule. In this fire they burn nine sacred woods, each with their own magical and spiritual attributes, as a way of calling those properties into their lives as they celebrate the return of light.

For some modern Pagans, Yule is first and foremost a celebration of community. At a time of year that is (at least for some of us) cold, dark, and (for a great many of us) tremendously stressful, we create an oasis of support and social warmth. In particular, many Queer Pagans find themselves struggling with exclusion from their blood family's celebrations, or, if they're not openly Queer, having to hide their true selves through holiday gatherings. Giving each other even just one night to gather and celebrate in an open and accepting space can make a tremendous difference in how we tolerate the literally and often metaphorically darkest part of the year. Yule is an opportunity to find comfort in chosen family, strengthen the bonds between yourself and those you love, and know that you are not alone.

On the other hand, Yule is also an excellent time to contemplate solitude and darkness. While the winter solstice is most commonly observed with focused hope and anticipation of returning light, it is also the longest night of the year. Just as the summer solstice can be celebrated as the peak of light, the winter solstice can be celebrated as the peak of darkness.

Depression is an all too common affliction in the winter months. There are no quick fixes, no simple rituals to suddenly make a depressed person feel better; to suggest such a thing would be an insult to anyone who has ever lived with depression. For some people, celebrating with a warm, welcoming community at Yule can make depression seem even worse—everything you could possibly want is right there, so why aren't you happy? Sometimes what a person needs is not cheering up, but acknowledgment and acceptance. On the longest night of the year we can find power in taking time to sit alone in the dark with ourselves and acknowledging our ugly moments. Seeing these struggles as real challenges, true battles for survival, allows us to recognize our strength in persevering through them. We do not have to win. We do not have to feel good. We do not have to deny the ache or the void. We see them, we salute them, and we defy them. The dark can devour us and become us, but still we exist, and its power becomes our power.

Feeling the pressure of the longest night and anticipating the return of light in longer days can have a visceral reality for people who suffer from seasonal affective disorder. For these individuals the need for light is a physical craving that affects every part of their mind, body, and spirit. Filling the ritual room with full-spectrum lights would be an effective but expensive way to help coven members with SAD get a midwinter boost, and could serve as a sort of electronic sacred Yule fire.

That said, there is something magical about gathering together around a real fire, whether it's a massive bonfire outside, or a tiny blaze lit in a cauldron indoors. A shared fire speaks to our most ancient roots as a species, and helps us build important community bonds. If your coven struggles with the physical challenges of dark winters, consider creating a customized sacred Yule fire. Instead of the traditional nine woods, choose woods and herbs that your coven associates with perseverance, joy, and optimism. Create a bright blaze, and draw those energies into you so that they can help you "power through" until spring.

Yule is often regarded as an optimal time to perform divination regarding the coming year. For some, this is interconnected with the quiet reflection and introspection of winter months. As we continue on our endless journey of understanding and expressing ourselves, Yule can be a good time to look into the metaphorical mirror, contemplate who we once were and how that might be different from who we are, and consider who we want to become. Divination can give us insight as to the challenges and advantages before us, as well as hints for how to find the bits of identity we hide even from ourselves.

While introspection divination is most often practiced in solitude, they can also be brought into circle as a coven activity. The most obvious solution is to have coven members perform readings for each other, but there are other options as well. Queer Pagans are constantly battling with extreme pressures to either conform to social norms or explicitly reject them. Mainstream society tells us to dress and act in specific ways, Pagans debate endlessly about what other Pagans should or shouldn't do, and Queer and Trans communities have their own implicit and explicit ideas for what qualifies a person for being one of them. In the face of such intense pressure from every direction, a coven can tremendously empower its members by creating space for them to sit and introspect and reflect and divine and just *be* in whatever way they want to be in that moment. Some people need that period of *not* having to interact in any specific way or participate in any particular activity. Setting time aside in sacred space for members to do whatever they want with their community's unobtrusive support tells people that they are cherished not just as participating member of the group, but also as individuals with their own needs, goals, and limits.

Imbolc

Imbolc is a Gaelic festival traditionally celebrated around February 1st, and strongly associated with the Goddess Brigid. The holiday features themes of fire, purification, spring cleaning, domesticity, the beginnings of fertility, and weather divination; modern Neopagans typically incorporate many of the same themes. In the mythology of Traditional Wicca, at Imbolc the Goddess of the Witches departs from the underworld and begins Her return journey to the land of the living. Some covens light candles to help guide the Goddess back to our world.

For covens that live in colder climates, Imbolc takes place about when people are getting fed up with freezing temperatures, and need a little extra light and warmth in their lives. The days are visibly getting longer, but the weather is still bitterly cold, and people often crave a way to express and meet their need for something warmer and brighter. Surrounding ourselves with lit candles and reorganizing our homes can let us feel freshly renewed even when the earth around us is still frozen solid. Increased light has a concrete psychological impact, causing us to feel more energetic and alert, and many people enjoy the sense of tangible progress from actually doing something to get ready for spring, rather than just sitting and waiting for the weather to warm up.

For queer Pagans in particular, Imbolc can be a holiday about revelation, catharsis, and renewal. Yule's introspection can yield insights that demand attention, and the stillness of the solstice gives way to a need for action at Imbolc. As we continuously examine ourselves, we learn about how we change and who we become through the journey of our life experiences. Sometimes parts of our identity that were once ripe with meaning become stagnant or empty as we transform and grow; other times we may discover elements of our personality that only ever existed as a defense mechanism to help us survive, but as we become stronger, or as our circumstances change, we no longer need that particular piece of armor. Sometimes we find that all the dead skin we've shed in seeking our true selves finally cleared the way for us see something we've hidden from ourselves since childhood, something that was never really part of us at all, but is a weight we've carried and can finally let go. While Imbolc's external spring cleaning gives us an active way to energize ourselves and prepare for changing seasons, Imbolc's internal spring cleaning clears out emotional deadfall and prunes back dying branches, giving us space for unhindered new growth.

Letting go can be the most difficult stage of personal transformation. Even when we know a relationship is toxic, it can be hard to leave, and this is true whether we're talking about relationships with others or relationships with ourselves. Covens can use an Imbolc ritual to support each other as they say those hard goodbyes and divorce themselves of what they no longer need. A somewhat traditional way of going about this could be writing the things you want to get rid of on a piece of paper, and then burning those papers in a sacred fire. If your group prefers something more spontaneous or freeform, simply standing in a circle and letting each member speak or shout or sing or laugh "I'm not _____ anymore!" gives the same opportunity for release with community support.

Having cleared the way for new potential to manifest, Imbolc is an excellent time to shed light on elements of ourselves that are newly discovered, and share them with a supportive community. As we continuously seek to know ourselves better, we will discover pieces of our identity we never saw before. Perhaps the piece you find is a newly shaped element of who you are, or perhaps you are only just now able to acknowledge what it is. Maybe you find something you were already familiar with now demands expression in an entirely new way.

Whatever you discover and desire to express, lighting candles in circle can become a ritual act of shared illumination in both a literal and metaphorical sense. Each member can reveal an aspect of themselves they've chosen to share with their coven as they light a candle to represent it. The candles themselves could even vary in color, size, and shape, which thankfully does not need to mean extra expense, as colored candles in different sizes are widely available in affordable options. Coven members could bring to ritual a specific candle that fits what they want to share with their group, or perhaps a candle for each revelation if you encourage people to share more than one. These lit candles then serve as both a magical act of shedding light upon once hidden elements of ourselves, as well as an act of communal recognition. If you wrote down and burned elements of self you needed to let go, consider using that fire to light your candles as a way of representing how clearing out and making space supports new development.

Once again, flames and candles are only one way to work with Imbolc's energetic tide of "out with the old, in with the new". If your group is less formal, perhaps all you need is a shared meal over which you can discuss what you've learned over the winter and how you want to move forward with that knowledge. If your group tends to be more active, perhaps you go somewhere or do something together dressed up as the people you want to be, outwardly manifesting your visions for yourselves as a way of saying to the world, "This is who I am!"

For a community that often spends so much time and energy hiding who we really are to get by in a world of privilege and intolerance, expressing ourselves without reservation, and being seen with not just tolerance but true acceptance, can be validating and empowering. We support and nourish the revelations of others by embracing their light, and in being given space and support to shine as our own true selves, we are better able to illuminate others in their quests for self expression.

Ostara

The vernal or spring equinox is commonly celebrated under the Anglo-Saxon name Ostara, taken from the name of a Germanic goddess named Eostre, who also inspired word for Easter in some languages, and was likely a manifestation of a Proto-Indo-Esuropean Goddess of dawn. Eostre was celebrated with a festival in early spring, which likely influenced celebrations for both Easter and the modern Pagan spring equinox. In the mythology of traditional Wicca, the Goddess of the Witches arrives in the land of the living at Ostara, tides of new life and regrowth returning with Her.

Even at latitudes where green shoots and colorful blossoms are still a month away, Ostara is a festival of spring. The most common way of observing Ostara is by literally planting seeds for new growth. Pagans in New England—where it is often still too cold to plant in the ground—participate by planting seeds indoors, either as potted plants or in biodegradable seeding cups to be moved outside when the earth is warm enough.

By physically participating in the natural currents of birth and regrowth, we align ourselves with that tide and welcome its energy into our lives. We can then ride the power of spring's growth to help us achieve our personal goals. Many Pagans imbue their seeds with the intent of something they want to manifest in their lives, with the intent that the thing they desire will grow with their plant. Some harness the transformative power of spring by putting imbuing the soil with whatever they must sacrifice in order to achieve their goals, or by using the dirt to represent a traumatic event and the seeds to represent personal growth that can arise from it. This can be accomplished by various means, including energetically charging the dirt, mixing a few drops of bodily fluids into the dirt, or writing your intent on a piece of paper, burning the paper, and mixing the ash with the dirt. The idea is to let the plant sprouting in soil become a sympathetic talisman for constructive change.

Ostara's planting, however, need not be entirely literal. At Imbolc we got a better sense of who we want to become, but how do we actually get there? Life often isn't as easy as "just do it". We need the means to achieve our desires, so planting metaphorical seeds at Ostara can mean preparing our lives and ourselves for what we want to accomplish. Spring's growth is about not just seeds and sprouts, but also the soil in which we sow our seeds. In this way, Ostara is an excellent time for Queer Pagans to examine privilege.

Whenever we attempt anything, our privilege or lack thereof determines our foundation. Attempting something that mainstream society regards as normal is like planting a seed in fertile soil at the optimum temperature. You don't need to worry as much about creating a conducive environment because the environment is already conducive; that is the very nature of privilege. When attempting something that is not the social norm, or attempting something entirely normal but as a marginalized or disenfranchised individual, you're planting in hard soil that's too hot or too cold, or has the wrong pH for your seed. Creating an environment that will nourish your goal becomes a necessity, and coven support becomes a stronger statement for equity in general. Looking critically at our metaphorical soil can show us both where we want to seek aid from our community, and where we have resources we can offer in support of others. Progress in any direction must begin with understanding.

As an equinox, Ostara brings with it an energy of inherent equality. For one day, everywhere on the Earth experiences nearly the same amount of light and dark. It is a great equalizer, and its energy can help us strive towards our goal with a fair chance. Effective magic is often a combination of ritual, spellcraft, and real life work. If your coven decides to use seeds and dirt for planting magic, consider following up with more mundane forms of effort and community support. For example:

❖ One person's goal is to dress masculine more often as a way to better express their gender. Their metaphorical planting is organizing their wardrobe so that when they're ready to wear masculine clothing, they don't have to fight with their closet to find it. Their coven supports the process by going through outfits with them and offering opinions on which items read more masculine, which seem more feminine, and which could go either way.

❖ A woman who just realized she is a lesbian decides to explore her sexual orientation by seeking a partner. She sets up a profile on a dating website, finds a local club with a gay night, and comes up with ideas for fun dates should she meet a woman she likes. Her coven supports her by having conversations with her about what she's looking for in a partner and what she wants out of a relationship, so that when she meets interested women she can better communicate her own desires.

❖ A person wants to find a new job with a better work environment. They prepare by searching job sites, putting together a resume, and learning how to identify a healthy workplace. Their coven supports them by offering feedback on their resume and cover letter, providing references, and giving mock-interviews for practice.

Another, albeit perhaps less common, theme in modern Pagan Ostara rituals is embracing one's inner child. Coloring books, hopscotch, jump rope, and reading picture books are just a few activities that people use to reconnect with their childhood. As Queer Pagans, this can be a chance to do the things we were pressured or scolded away from when we were little. It might seem a little silly, particularly to groups with a more somber approach to ritual, but that silliness is part of the point. In order to move forward as adults, we must remember to listen for our child selves, and what better time to nourish those parts of us that were suppressed or neglected than at Ostara? If preparing the means to achieve our goals is fertilizing the soil in which we plant our seeds, then making time to laugh and play is aerating the soil, for it is difficult to grow anything in that hard-packed dirt.

Beltane

Beltane is about fertility, creativity and sex. Its name is taken from the Gaelic May Day festival held on May 1st, but our modern Pagan Beltane is likely influenced more by the Germanic May Day festivals. In the mythology of traditional Wicca, Beltane celebrates the sexual union of the Goddess and God of the witches, and in contemporary Paganism sex and fertility continue to be the holiday's most prominent themes. Beltane is also both counterpoint and partner to Samhain, being the other hinge of the year, when life flows into the world rather than out.

The most common contemporary Beltane activity by far is the maypole. A tall pole is erected in the earth with ribbons attached to the top. An even number of people grab ribbons, then dance around the pole in a manner which weaves the ribbons against it. The dance is an act of fertility magic, meant to help new life return to the earth, as well as to the dancers themselves. Most Pagan groups practice fertility magic of some variety at Beltane, and the "new life" it brings can be interpreted in many ways. Some people hope for the fertility for their farms or gardens, or for themselves if they wish to conceive a child. Others think more metaphorically of bringing "new life" to a dull subject, and want fresh creativity in their work, or renewed inspiration in their art. Beltane is an excellent time to focus on what you manifest in the world, and let the tides of seasonal energy enhance whatever you do.

The maypole dance is intentionally phallic, and in some modern Pagan groups this symbolism is emphasized as much as possible: women dig a hole in the earth and decorate it with flowers, while men find or prepare an appropriate pole; the men then approach the women with their pole, and seductively convince them to allow the pole into their hole. The cisgendered and heterosexual bias is immediately apparent, and extremely problematic for Queer Pagans. Some groups handle this by allowing anyone who identifies as a man prepare the pole, while anyone who identifies as a woman prepares the hole. While this is an improvement, it still leaves us with a problematic binary. One group tackles the binary problem by inviting people who identify as anything other than a man or a woman to form a chain between those two groups, physically and metaphorically bringing them together. For this community, their solution is deeply meaningful, as many of them see other-gendered people as a bridge between binary genders, and they enjoy a ritualized way to represent their sacred work. Other Queer Pagans have found this solution dissatisfying, as it seems to show other-gendered people as mere facilitators for heterosexual union, and they crave representations of sex and fertility without any binary at all.

Thankfully, nature provides us with plenty of examples of fertility and procreation that are not strictly heterosexual (by which I mean that their gender roles defy a strict binary, and the sexes of the creatures involved are more complex than simply male and female, even when genetically their reproduction is still a union of two gametes). Trees, flowers with their bee co-conspirators, snails, seahorses, certain primates, and many other creatures give us examples of natural sexual activity without binary sex or binary gender, and can be creatively represented in ritual.

For example, one year our group chose to mimic snail sex at Beltane for our fertility and creativity magic. Most land snails are hermaphroditic, and pairs reproduce by spearing each other with "love darts" (yes, this is what they are actually called, although the technical term is *gypsobelum*) and exchanging sperm. We all wore plain white T-shirts acquired for the occasion, and used pool noodles covered in body paint to lance each other with our creative energy. The ritual was fun and messy and inevitably ended with people consensually rubbing up against each other to "share the love". The brightly painted T-shirts became talismans for creative magic. Some people kept their shirt to wear when they needed an extra boost of creativity. Others cut up their shirt and used the fabric to create works of art and magic.

For many Pagans, Beltane is also about the visceral pleasure of sexual activity. Paganism generally regards physical and spiritual realities as equally sacred, so enjoying your body and its pleasures can be a sacred act. Certainly enjoyment of the flesh could include sound, taste, smell, and any other sensation, sexual or otherwise, but with Beltane's overwhelming theme of fertility, sexual pleasure takes center stage. Many groups and communities celebrate by engaging in activities ripe with sexual innuendo, whereas some consummate with actual sex itself. Of course, what constitutes "sex" is difficult to define, so even in a group where sexual activity is welcome as part of ritual observance, it is important to define exactly what actions that includes.

Perhaps because of this semantic ambiguity, Beltane often brings up the subject of consent. Many modern Pagans are often eager to hug, touch, and energetically connect without first gaining explicit consent. There seems to be an underlying notion that intent is all that really matters, and as long as you were trying to help or do good for someone, they should be grateful, even if they didn't want or ask for what you gave them. This idea that intent is what really matters arises from certain Western approaches to magic, where the outpouring of will is what makes a thing work, rather than the specific mechanisms of how one expresses that will. Unfortunately, this thinking only holds true so long as the subject of that will is not an entity with agency. As soon as you start affecting something or someone with their own ideas, wants, and limits, your intent only matters so far.

In the context of Beltane, this means that just because you like hugs doesn't mean that every other person will like them, or want one, or want one from you. People must develop better habits of asking for consent with explicit language: just because groping isn't "sex" for you doesn't mean it won't be "sex" for them, so agreements like "we can mess around as long as we don't have sex" generally aren't clear enough without previously established and mutually shared definitions. It's also helpful to decide beforehand just how sexual you want the energy of your ritual to get, and make sure all participants are comfortable with that intensity. Being part of a ritual with tons of sexual energy you weren't expecting can feel a little like being at an orgy and being pressured to participate even if you don't want to.

Of course, sometimes things change in the heat of the moment. A participant might suddenly decide that the activity they agreed to isn't what they really want at all, and they should be allowed to make a graceful exit. Consider setting aside a space for aftercare, where people can go to ground, center, and transition from sacred space to mundane awareness. When someone wants to bow out of the ritual, having a designated place to go gives them a sense of support and validation—the group must be OK with them leaving the activity because a way is provided to do so.

On the other hand, sometimes a ritual gets a little steamier than intended, and it's useful to have ways to engage with those rising energies without coercion or consent violations. Asking for consent does not need to interrupt your ritual. In fact, intentionally including requests for consent is an important way to show that your community respects and values its members. Rubbing up against each other was not part of our original Beltane snail sex ritual plan. Delighted and excited by our activity, one participant approached another and asked, "Can I rub my paint on you?" Their tone was light-hearted, and their body language expressed interest without pressure. They indicated with a gesture exactly which patch of paint they wanted to rub on the other person, and they asked from a comfortable distance so that they weren't already invading personal space with the question. The other person could easily have said no, and the ritual would have continued jovially. This is true partly because the questioner, being someone who values consent enough to ask for it, is also someone who will gracefully respect a refusal, and partly because our community has intentionally created an atmosphere where asking for consent is the norm, and "no" is always an acceptable answer.

For Queer Pagans, Beltane can be a holiday of penultimate personal expression. It's a day to joyfully proclaim your sex, let your gender shine however you please, and enjoy those with whom you share mutual attraction. As your group plans its Beltane celebration, ask yourselves what you want to manifest, what fuels your creativity, and how you want to enjoy your flesh.

Litha

A celebration of light, power, and partnership, modern Paganism observes the summer solstice under the name Litha, taken from the Anglo-Saxon name for the first summer month. In traditional Wicca, Litha honors the sacred marriage of the Goddess and God of the Witches, and celebrates the height of the power of light. It also marks another battle between the Oak and Holly Kings, this time with Holly as the victor, heralding the coming dark. Summer solstice celebrations occur all over the world, and take many fascinating forms that are not always religious or even spiritual in nature. A group looking for inspiration outside the Wiccan myth cycle will have plenty to draw from.

Litha is a time to celebrate strength, climax, and manifestation. The sun's tremendous power has an undeniable impact on our planet, and on the summer solstice we revel in its energy. Some Pagans observe the solstice with rituals that celebrate the Sun, others with dances around bonfires, and others by using the Sun's energy to charge magical acts and objects. Midsummer's energy can be seen as a tremendous spotlight; there is no better time to put the things you want on center stage. With the Sun at the height of its power, we bring ourselves and our desires into the light of day.

On June 28th, 1969, a group of lesbian, gay, bisexual, transgender, and queer people rioted following a police raid on a gay bar at the Stonewall Inn in New York City. The following year people commemorated the event with Gay Pride parades in New York, Los Angeles, San Francisco, and Chicago. From there the Gay Pride movement spread across the world, bringing with it a surge of political activism.

While Gay Pride parades do not always take place in June, the vast majority do, honoring and remembering the Stonewall Riots. If Litha is about bringing things to light and manifesting your desire, and Gay Pride is about representing LGBTQ+ identity and demanding equal rights for all, then celebrating both together can feel like a natural connection for Queer Pagans. Litha and Gay Pride both are times for coming out and being out, for letting your true self shine, for manifesting the self you want to be and the world you want to live in.

That said, just as it is important for us to recognize the value of activists who put their lives on the line to achieve social justice, and recognize the importance of their work to increase visibility for our community, we must also acknowledge that it is not only necessary but right for some individuals to refrain from being publicly visible as part of the LGBTQ+ community. Coming out must be a choice, and if we insist that everyone "should" be out, then that choice is less a choice and more a path coerced on us by a community that oversimplifies complex issues and generalizes political ideals onto individual lives. It is possible to say that we want a future where everyone can be "out" about who they are with no negative ramifications, and yet still support individual privacy in the present. When we take away a person's choice about whether or not to be "out", we weaken our own foundations—it is not truly a choice if it can only be made one way.

Queer Pagans who are "in the closet" can still work with Litha's tides of brilliance and exhibition. Our presentation does not necessarily need to match our identity. It certainly can be a liberating expression of who we are, but it can also be a carefully crafted persona, a tool designed to help us get what we need to survive as a healthy and happy being. Modern Paganism tends to cringe at the idea of outwardly being anything other than what we truly are, yet we don't flinch at the general concept of wearing a suit to a job interview, even if we'd never want to wear one to anything else. The real problem of charlatans in Neopagan spirituality has left us with baggage around concepts of identity that bias us against anything that can be even remotely construed as disingenuous. Certainly there are many arenas in which discernment and skepticism are necessary tools with which we arm ourselves against impostors and frauds, but we must not let this fear completely turn us away from utilizing our personal presentation as a tool with which we work our will. Our will is, after all, an element of our identity, and thus any expression of it speaks to our true nature.

A Litha ritual, then, can be anything from a publicly spectacular display of spirituality and identity, to a private and focused magical working aimed at creating a public face that will ease the way towards a certain goal. For example:

❖ A coven decides to celebrate Litha by attending their city's Pride parade as a group. To add a little magic to their outing, they each make a necklace out of beads in rainbow colors, and meet on the day of the solstice to charge their necklaces in circle with the power of the Sun. They wear their necklaces when they go to Pride, so that the energy they captured in ritual can help boost visibility and add momentum to the cause of LGBTQ+ rights.

❖ A coven exploring the relationship between identity and presentation uses Litha as a day to experiment with expressing hidden elements of themselves in safe space. In a private circle they proudly come out as whoever and whatever they are, and experience what it feels like to be visible to a community. At the end of the ritual, they reflect on whether or not they wish to maintain this new aspect of their presentation in their everyday life.

❖ A coven that chooses to blend in with a socially conservative area for the safety of its members crafts a spell specifically aimed at promoting an image of normalcy to onlookers. Each person presents an image of themselves as an average, harmless, and decent member of the civic community so that they can continue living their private lives unmolested.

It is worth noting here that magic designed around creating an image of yourself will be infinitely more effective if it is based on some substantial truth, and can be somewhat dangerous otherwise. In the final example, a person who genuinely wishes no harm to come to their neighbor, and simply wants to live their own life with the same freedoms as the next person will find it easy to harness the energy of the Sun to promote an image of themselves as peaceful and harmless. That is, after all, a true sentiment within them, even if their neighbor might contextualize it differently. Someone who attempts to use summer solstice energy to promote themselves as harmless while secretly planning violence might suddenly find their deceptive nature brought to light.

Just as Yule honors both the power of dark and the coming light, Litha honors both the power of light and the coming dark. The summer solstice can feel like the beginning of summer, with the heat of July and August still ahead, but steadily lengthening nights remind us that summer's time is limited. We must enjoy light's power while it is in surplus, because soon the dark will be upon us whether we are ready for it or not. Some covens might choose to charge candles with solar energy at Litha, saving them to burn in the winter when sunlight becomes sparse, or to use in a Yule circle as a way of calling back the Sun. An awareness of coming dark at Litha can motivate us to treasure the power of light and use it to prepare ourselves for what lies ahead. We can craft our presentation like a set of armor, and be ready to face the future with strength manifested from within and powered from above.

Lammas

Lammas, now celebrated in modern Paganism on August 1st, takes its name for the Anglo-Saxon *hlaf-mas*, meaning loaf mass, a festival celebrating the first grain harvest with specially baked bread. The Neopagan Lammas is also heavily influenced by the Gaelic Lughnasadh, another first-fruits festival, which involved games and competition. Some modern Pagans celebrate their holiday under the name Lughnasadh or Lughnasa. In the mythology of Traditional Wicca, at Lammas the Goddess sacrifices the God to fertilize the Earth and feed Their people.

In our coven, Lammas is about sacrifice. We celebrate the things we endure and give up in order to get what we want. We look deep into loss and suffering, and learn what it can teach us about each other and about ourselves.

As we travel through life, we constantly reshape ourselves in the context of who we were, who we are, and who we want to become. At times this transformational process can be a peaceful emergence of one thing from the last, or a joyful discovery with exuberant expression. Just as often, however, we grow through anguish, whether by enduring something terrible as the price for something we want, or by giving up something precious to make room for something we've deemed more important.

Lammas urges us to ask ourselves hard questions about what we need to do in order to get what we want and become who we want to be. What are you willing to give up to attain your desire? How hard are you willing to work toward your goal? How much are you willing to suffer for what you want? Sometimes these exchanges are direct and obvious—someone wants a degree but must work two miserable jobs on top of school to pay their way through it; someone wants a new job but must move across the country, leaving friends and family behind, in order to take it; someone wants to make a special purchase, but must significantly trim their budget and forgo other purchases in order to save enough money.

Sometimes the exchange is not so straightforward. Someone wants to join a choir and become a better singer; it doesn't seem like they have to give up anything to do that, but going to rehearsal twice a week and making time to practice at home means less time to spend with friends or lovers, less time to pursue other hobbies, and less time to relax and manage stress. The individual may well decide that the exchange is well worth it, that singing in choir feeds their soul in a necessary way that more than makes up for what they loose from it, but that cost is still there, and it's important to recognize. If we close our eyes to these natural costs, then someday we might suddenly see all we've lost to get where we are, and bitterness can spoil our sense of achievement. By making a conscious choice to recognize the prices we pay, we empower our actions with that value, and put ourselves in a position of strength for future reflection.

Every day we make these kinds of choices, giving up one thing so that we can have another. Sometimes the things we shed can be items, activities, relationships, or elements of ourselves that no longer serve us, that hold us back from who and what we want to be. Some would argue that giving up these things is not truly a sacrifice, since they needed to go anyway. I find that this is true only when you see both the meaning of the word "sacrifice" and the sacrifice you make in a very binary sort of way—it's all good or all bad, all necessary or all unnecessary.

I'll offer my divorce as an example. There were plenty of ways in which my marriage was bad for me. The relationship was unhealthy, and our domestic arrangement held me back from the life I wanted to live. Getting rid of that seems less like a sacrifice and more like purification ... except that I loved my then-husband. There was plenty about our relationship that was good, and there were things about how we lived together that I will miss for the rest of my life. I will never have any of those things again, and I knew that when I walked out the door. It hurt, and it still hurts, but it's worth it. It's a sacrifice I made to become who I am, and while I certainly look back, it's with gratitude, not regret.

That act of looking back seems to be another point of controversy for some, particularly when we're talking about the painful struggles of discovering who we are and casting aside elements that keep us from our true selves. For many, a "dead-name" (a name no longer held that represents a discarded identity) is just that: dead. Revisiting it in any way is nothing more than a cause for unnecessary pain and suffering, and forcing someone to confront a "dead-name" is always disrespectful and unacceptable. That said, at Lammas an individual might choose to look back on their "dead-name" and their former self to recognize what was lost in their transition. The point is not to say that their former self was good and they never should have given it up, but rather to acknowledge that sometimes even though something has goodness in it, we still must walk away.

Some might argue that there is little point in revisiting that hurt, as having lived it once is enough, but I offer history as an example to the contrary. Consider the public opinion on women's suffrage in 1845 as Margaret Fuller published *Woman in the Nineteenth Century*, in 1920 as the nineteenth amendment passed, in the 1980s when women finally be-

gan to equal men in voter turnout, and yet again in the insanity that was
the 2016 presidential election. At each point in time, women's right to
vote took on a very different meaning, from something prohibited to
something new and controversial to something almost taken for granted,
and then to something once again at the center of controversy. As context
changes, so does the way in which we consider elements of our past, the
manifestation of our present, and our goals for the future. Periodically
looking back on the sacrifices we've made to get where we are allows us to
appreciate the work we've done in new and important ways, and to avoid
repeating mistakes we've made in the past.

As Coven Craft is about working in a group, Lammas is an excellent
time to look also at community sacrifice. Consider public activists who
give up time and energy and sometimes risk their own personal safety to
campaign for equal rights. Recognize the members of your group who do
unglamorous work behind the scenes, or complete unpleasant tasks because it's necessary for the well-being of the coven. Celebrate those who
are willing to take a phone call from a distraught covener at three a.m.,
even though it means being exhausted the next day, because they're willing
to give up a little of their own comfort to give comfort to someone else.
Be cautious, however, about how you treat the social dynamics of community service. The sacrifices we make for others, big and small, are powerful
acts of support when given willingly, but when performed with a grudging
sense of duty, they become hollow and divisive. Different people will support your group in different ways. Not everyone *can* take that three a.m.
call, so make sure that's not the only kind of service your group appreciates.
Look at the way in which every member contributes to the whole, and
celebrate each other inclusively.

A traditional Wiccan Lammas ritual involve baking bread in the shape
of a man, representing the God of the Witches, which is cut and eaten to
represent His sacrifice to feed the Earth and its inhabitants. The act of
making bread and sharing it as a community has a long and rich history in
all corners of human culture, and certainly it can be adapted in many ways
for Neopaganism. Your bread can take any shape that feels appropriate for
your group, and you could add symbolic meaning to it by seasoning it with
appropriate herbs. For groups that lack a resident baker, store-bought

bread can be charged with intent in circle. Some groups don't use bread at all, but instead create a "first fruits"-type offering of seasonal produce typical of early fall in their area. Both activities convey of sense of effort, sacrifice, and mutual nourishment.

Other groups go an entirely different route, sacrificing objects of personal value. One of the most memorable Lammas rituals I ever attended as a young Pagan involved every group member choosing something to give up as an act of solidarity with all those who sacrifice for our benefit. One person created a beautiful full-color drawing; another wrote something that no one else would ever read; another chose a string of pearls with deep personal significance. Each item was unique and carried meaning for the individual. We consecrated our objects in circle, then as a group we went to the local river and cast them into the water. It was surprisingly difficult to watch our treasures disappear, but that was the point. If it were easy, it wouldn't mean anything.

To truly be ourselves—our full selves, no more and no less—is often difficult. At Lammas we honor challenge and suffering, and in doing so we celebrate worth and strength.

Mabon

The autumnal or fall equinox is commonly known as Mabon in modern Paganism. The name comes from Mabon ap Modron, a character from Welsh mythology whose name translates to "Son of the Great Mother." Sometime around 1970, Aidan Kelly proposed finding or assigning "Pagan names" for the vernal equinox, summer solstice, and autumnal equinox. As mentioned above, Kelly's names for Ostara and Litha make a great deal of sense, and Ostara in particular seems more like a rediscovery than an invention. Mabon, on the other hand, continues to be a mysterious choice, despite its persisting popularity.

Mabon is essentially a Pagan Thanksgiving. It's a time to express gratitude for the things we have and cherish, and in doing so create a little sympathetic magic to ensure those things are plentiful in the coming year. The traditional Pagan Mabon is about literal nourishment—the food we eat provided by the Earth we live on. It's a time to recognize the interplay between life and death, and to thank the plants and animals that die to feed us. Of course, the best way to celebrate food is with a feast, so the central feature of a Mabon ritual is typically a large meal, often pot-luck, with participants contributing favorite foods.

Some groups coordinate their meals with precision, ensuring that every food group is represented, and essential staples (like coffee and chocolate) are in copious supply. Some might want to ensure that all foods are locally acquired, organic, free range, and seasonally appropriate, so that the meal itself respects the Earth as it celebrates it. Others groups take a more laid-back approach, with each member choosing whatever they want to bring, whether it's homemade, store-bought, or simply the best they had to offer. These groups let the general intent of their feast speak louder than the specific foods presented, which is often more practical for smaller covens, as well as for covens for which preparing a large and expensive feast is not feasible or even possible. A feast of cheese and crackers can be a powerful ritual of thanksgiving if that's what you have and you enjoy it with genuine gratitude.

One year very early in my Pagan career, I found myself without a coven to celebrate Mabon. I decided to host a Mabon-themed dinner with my non-Pagan but wonderfully open-minded friends instead, and sent them an invitation email with a general explanation of what they should bring to the pot-luck: something they wanted to make sure they'd have enough of for the following year. One of my friends was a talented marksman, and he brought ... bullets. We all delighted in how he interpreted the invitation, and we put the bullets on the table with the food and gave thanks for all of it. At the time it seemed funny in a very appropriate way, but the more I thought about it, the more sense it made. Why not give thanks for everything? Certainly food and physical nourishment and our dependency on the Earth can take center stage, but why not express gratitude for other things as well? Why not make Mabon a festival of gratitude in a very general sense?

Today our coven celebrates Mabon with two expressions of gratitude. One is our feast, which is more elaborate in some year and less so in others. The other is a ritual we designed to show the interplay between gratitude and gratification—for it is our ability to enjoy that which we have that allows us to appreciate that which we get. In our ritual we create a shrine or altar upon which each member places representations of the things they want for or in the coming year—objects, goals, concepts, accomplishments, attitudes, or anything else a person desires, represented by items, pictures, writing, or whatever else the individual deems appropriate. Each member then writes on a piece of paper what they are thankful for. Participants are invited to share their gratitude with the group if they choose, but it's not a requirement. Some members write long expressions of appreciation, and speak only a single item from their list, and that's OK too. Then everyone places their paper in a fireproof container, and we burn them together, feeling the power of our gratitude in the heat of the flames. Then we light a candle from those flames, and place it on the altar of our desires, using its power to drive us toward our goals.

Mabon's expressions of gratitude need not, and perhaps should not, be exclusively internal. Whether you're inspired by Mahatma Gandhi's urge to "be the change you want to see in the world", or by Robin Chase's advice to "create the world you want to live in", by performing acts of charity we become the gratitude and gratification we seek. Food donations are the most obvious and perhaps typical example of a Mabon charity. Consecrating items for donation in circle, imbuing them with energy for satisfaction and success, is a straightforward way to become an agent of gratitude.

That said, just as our desires are often nonmaterial, such as goals we strive towards, skills we want to learn, or attitudes we want to adopt, charity too can take the form of action rather than object. Your coven may choose to donate time and effort to a cause that speaks to your group, or you might support each other as each individual chooses their own charity project to pursue. Everyone can act, and no action is too small. Whatever your group's resources, and whatever your personal resources, you can find some way to volunteer for a cause that matters to you. If you're not sure how to begin, search online for organizations that support your goals or ideals. Many organizations have instructions on their website for how to get involved as a volunteer, but if they don't, call and ask.

Like the vernal equinox, the autumnal equinox is an equalizer, with almost everywhere on earth experiencing nearly the same amount of light and darkness. We give thanks in that moment of equality, not when spring's bounty is about to fulfill us, but when we know that the cold dark of winter lies ahead. We give thanks for what resources we have to face that winter, and we give thanks to show that we can experience gratitude in the face of adversity, for that capacity to appreciate ourselves and our lives becomes our power to persevere.

Creating Your Own Holidays

Some people won't like the idea of participating in the eight Sabbats made prevalent by Wicca, and that's OK. Each group must make its own decision both about whether or not celebrating holidays is something they want to do at all, and, if it is, which holidays they want to celebrate. Those answers will vary as much as the groups themselves. If your group chooses not to observe the traditional Sabbats, but still wants special days to commemorate with ritual, consider creating your own coven calendar with occasions that have meaning for your members. The following questions can help guide your process:

❖ Which days are important to your group? National holidays? Historical dates? Anniversaries of significant events in social justice? The founding of your group, or special dates in your coven's formation or history?

❖ Why are your days important to you? What do they mean, and what do you hope to get out of revisiting them each year?

❖ What ritual actions would appropriately express your intent? Do you want to play the same ice-breaking game you played when your group gathered for the first time? Do you want to work magic towards a goal related to the holiday you chose? Do you want to perform community service that contributes to the theme of the day?

Annual celebrations can be both a bonding and stabilizing factor for any group. Certainly covens must exist that can pick holidays as they go and create new rituals for each one, and the ritual designer in me finds that concept liberating and exciting. That said, the coven leader in me shudders at the thought of all that logistical planning having to be recreated from scratch for each occasion. When life gets hectic (for example, during winter holidays), even participating in a new ritual can seem like a drain on emotional resources that are already in short supply—what will it be like? How do they need to prepare? What will they need for processing their experience afterward? Having a familiar holiday lets people relax and feel more comfortable participating, even if the ritual itself is a new take on a known theme, because, at the very least in a general sense, people know what they're in for. That familiarity engenders comfort.

Taking an even wider view, annual celebrations of any sort give groups a sense of common identity and investment in the continuation of their community. The holiday office party serves the same social function as the anniversary gala, which is also part of every religious holiday: celebrating the same event together year after year makes people feel like they are part of a persisting community.

Of course, if something new comes up that your group wants to celebrate, by all means, make a ritual for it! We can mix annual holidays with new and unique celebrations, offering our groups a mixture of creative spontaneity and long term stability. Just remember to keep practicality in mind as you design your calendar: How often can your group meet? How many of those meetings do you want to be holidays? How many of those holidays do you want to be the same every year? Balance your numbers at the start so that you don't end up halfway through the year with everyone already exhausted from too much ritual.

Magic

Magic, sometimes spelled "magick" in order to differentiate it from illusion and magic tricks, is famously defined by Aleister Crowley as "the Science and Art of causing Change to occur in conformity with Will." (*Magick in Theory and Practice*. Crowley, Aleister, 1991). His definition is intentionally broad, allowing for everything from taking out the trash to complex spellcraft to qualify as "magic". In this paradigm, magic is not some separate force that works while the magician idly waits for manifestation. Magic is instead a dynamic within the magician, a force at work within every action. Magical power comes from a union of will in all spheres of one's life, mystical, ritual, and practical. Harnessing that force means acknowledging your own power, and not just in a spiritual sense but in a mundane sense as well.

This empowerment is at the heart of why magic appears in nearly every form of Coven Craft, from the primarily religious and devotional to the nearly atheistic. Witchcraft, Wicca, and nearly every form of Neopaganism have at their center, whether declaratively or indirectly, some form of empowerment, be it from self-expression, enlightenment, strengthening relationships with the divine, or all of the above. In the broadest sense, all of these endeavors can be described as magic.

All that said, the term "magic" (or "magick") also finds colloquial use in describing mystical, spiritual, or ritual acts performed to achieve defined results. It is this particular subset of magic that we shall investigate in this chapter. The circle cast in Coven Craft has obvious ties to the circle of ceremonial magic, used either to contain raised energy, provide protection, or both. Our circle serves these purposes as well, providing us with safely warded space in which to work our magic, and containing energy we raise so that we can then direct it toward our goal.

Any venture into the world of magic should start with the fundamentals. We begin by becoming acquainted with our own power—how to enhance it, how to direct it, and how to maintain it ... or, in other words: energy work.

Energy Work

At various points I have mentioned gathering or directing energy, or charging an object with energy. As covered in the introduction, definitions of "energy" in this context vary widely, and thus defining what it means to direct energy or charge an object will be similarly varied. Assuming, however, that you have some personal definition of what energy is, and a belief that you can affect it, energy work is the practice of actually using it. In a sense, every act of ritual and magic can be considered energy work, but when we use that particular terminology we're generally referring to either fundamental energy skills, raising energy, manipulating energy, or directing energy.

Fundamental energy skills include grounding, centering, shielding, and tapping. Grounding takes its name from the earth beneath our feet, and from the electrical concept of a ground to direct excess energy away from a system to prevent it from being overloaded. When we ground ourselves in an energetic sense, we connect with an energy source larger than ourselves—usually the Earth itself, although there are exceptions—and use that connection both to stabilize our own energy and to act as an outflow for any excess energy we might need to shed. It is also possible to draw energy up from that connection, which is known as tapping, although it is possible to tap from any energy source, even when grounded into another.

Centering means aligning your mental focus and your energetic self or energy body with your physical form. When grounding, tapping, working magic, performing ritual, or any other energetically intense activity, it is easy to get caught up in the energy of what you're doing and lose your sense of where you are in relation to everything else. Centering is regaining your sense of context and maintaining an awareness of who, where, and what you are.

Shielding means creating a barrier of protective energy around yourself. Everyone emanates energy, and some people do it more "loudly" than others. Shields help us cut down on the amount of static we pick up just from being near another person. Generally speaking, a shield should be selectively permeable, allowing just enough energy to reach you, and filtering out anything that would be disruptive.

Energy fundamentals are tremendously difficult to teach through text. A number of exercises and visualizations to help you get started can be found in the appendix. Connecting breath with energy is tremendously common and frequently effective, particularly for people who tend to be kinesthetic learners; breathing in pulls energy towards you, and breathing out pushes it away. Visual learners will find more success imagining their energy as variously colored light, visualizing its shape and movement. Auditory learners might hear energy as a song that swells or quiets, changing in pitch or rhythm as it is directed one way or another. Some people experience energy as taste or smell, and those scents or flavors sometimes correspond with physical things such as vanilla or pine smoke, but sometimes have their own unique character. Some people feel energy like emotion. Still others have a sense that is entirely unique to metaphysical energy, and while it may also correspond with sound or taste or sight, that energy sense is its own unique experience.

The process of discovering how you perceive energy and how you can best direct energy is something that cannot be read about, but must be done. A teacher can help guide you through that process with exercises, experiments, and constructive feedback, but if you cannot find someone near you, make the attempt on your own. Try as many different techniques as you can think up until you find what works for you. Practice. When you think you've got that one skill mastered, keep practicing it. Even the most gifted adept still needs practice (in fact, a strong argument can be made for talented energy workers needing practice most of all, because a powerful weapon carelessly wielded is a danger to all).

When Neopagans talk about raising energy, they mean using one of many different possible methods to build up a large amount of energy to be used for a specific purpose. A recent trend in ecstatic-style Neopagan rituals has people raising energy and then just leaving it there, which is problematic in many ways. To begin with, it's somewhat disrespectful to wherever the energy came from. It took effort to raise that energy, so don't waste it. More concerning, though, is that raised energy simply left after ritual can cause complications after the fact. It might seem harmless enough to do your ecstatic dance of joy and then just leave the energy in that space when you're done, but someone might come along later who is sensitive to that energetic charge, and find themselves completely over-stimulated by what you left behind. The energy might seem pleasant to you, but there's no guarantee that the next person will perceive it the same way, or that it will be conducive to whatever happens next in that place. If your intent in raising energy is just to bask in the glow of what you raised, then at the very least make sure to clean it up before you leave.

Typically, raised energy is used to power a spell or a prayer, or to charge an item for magical use. Sometimes it is also offered up to a deity as a gift when that specific type of energy is somehow appropriate or relevant. "Charging" something essentially means pouring energy into it. The source of that energy can be summoned from within yourself (make sure you have a solid ground and be careful of depleting yourself), drawn up from a tapped source, or directed from energy raised in ritual. People most often talk about "charging" an object and "powering" a spell or a prayer, but this difference is effectively semantic. In all three, energy is directed at the goal to give it the power needed for success or fulfillment.

There are many, many ways of raising energy. The paths of power described below are ways of accessing and raising energy for ritual, magic, and worship, but there is another type of energy raising that doesn't fit well into any single path (it relates to at least two, those being connection and energy), and merits its own discussion regardless. This other type can be called interpersonal energy dynamics.

Two or more individuals working together can raise energy by focusing on the dynamics between them. Polarity is the most commonly used energy dynamic, and the principle upon which Wiccan magic and ritual in particular is founded. The power of polarity lies in embracing how opposites enhance and highlight one another. Tension, separation, and union between polar opposites all create surges of energy that can power ritual and magic. The polarity so common in Wicca focuses overwhelmingly on binary sex and gender, and while there is certainly power in that dynamic, we wanted to embrace other options. If the polar dynamics between male and female or woman and man work for you, then use them. Polarity based on binary sex and gender has been so thoroughly examined elsewhere that there is no reason to discuss it further here, but it bears repeating that we use other interpersonal energy dynamics in addition to polarity, not entirely in place of it.

Before moving on to those alternatives, however, we recognize that there are many other types of polarity to work with in magic and energy raising. We are all complex individuals, and there are many ways in which we complement each other in our differences. Working with dynamic polarity in circle means focusing on those differences and using the interplay between them to generate energy. Furthermore, polarity does not necessarily mean duality. Groups of people can explore the dynamics of opposition, difference, and cooperation among themselves to find polar dynamics that spread in multiple directions. The things we are *not* help us know who we *are*, and constructive contrast helps us shine.

Some differences are not oppositional at all, and combine to create something greater than the sum of their parts. This is the dynamic power of synergy. In synergy the traits of one individual enhance the traits of another, and vice versa. Imagine one coven member who loves to play the flute for musical magic, another who loves composing eloquent prayers, and a third who loves blending their own incense. There is nothing opposite or contrary about these approaches to ritual. They are different, but not in a polar way. Each is very capable of raising energy with their own methods, but when the flutist plays a melody while the poet speaks an incantation and the herbalist burns incense created for their purpose, the result of their efforts combined is something greater and more powerful than any single piece alone. Erotic magic can also function with synergy rather than polarity. Wherever you and your partner or partners exist on the various spectra of identity, using the ways in which your differences excite and delight each other raises synergistic energy.

Highlighting difference is not the only way to raise energy between individuals. Recognizing our similarities can be empowering with its sense of shared experience and solidarity. A group working with a shared belief in a common goal can raise energy with dynamic resonance in assenting voices. Homosexual sex magic can create magnificently powerful resonant energy. Any shared idea, emotion, experience, or identity can be a source of resonance. Polarity and synergy are about connection through difference, but resonance is about connection through similarity.

However you choose to engage with interpersonal energy dynamics, remember that people are complex and ever-changing. All of our relationships have elements of polarity, synergy, and resonance within each of them. There is no single dynamic that will always be right for certain people, but rather a focus that best suits your purpose at any given moment. Synergy might be the right dynamic for your group to use for one ritual, but resonance could be a better fit for another. A lesbian triad could work resonant sex magic for one occasion, polar sex magic for another, and synergistic sex magic for a third. Communicate with your group about how you think and feel within the context of your intent, and choose the dynamic that suits you best for that circle.

Sympathetic Magic

Sympathetic magic is perhaps the oldest form of magic. From Paleo-lithic cave paintings and hunting rituals to modern twinkle lights at the winter solstice, creating a representation of what we want as a focus for desire is nearly as old as humanity itself. The social anthropologist James Frazer (1890, *The Golden Bough: A Study in Magic and Religion,* abridged, illustrated, reprinted in 1998, New York: Oxford University Press) de-scribes sympathetic magic as functioning on two basic principles: similarity and contagion.

Similarity is the idea that like attracts like; any one thing will draw to it other things like it. Thus, by creating an image or representation of something you want, you increase the likelihood that the real thing will appear in your life. Some modern magicians believe that the force of simi-larity will actively attract what you desire. Other magicians believe that surrounding yourself with the energy of something makes it easier for you to manifest that thing. They might liken it to preparing soil with just the right nutrients and pH for the wildflower they want to grow. They'd argue that you can't always force a seed into your soil, but you can make certain that only the plant you want will thrive when it lands in your garden. An-other popular metaphor for how similarity functions is filling a pond by digging an aqueduct that directs water towards it; the magic doesn't call the rain, but it does direct the rain once it falls. Most magicians believe that some combination of attraction and facilitation account for sympa-thetic magic's effectiveness. Like attracts like, and the conducive environ-ment helps it thrive.

When considering how to represent your desire in an act of sympa-thetic magic, keep in mind the old saying, "You get what you ask for." Sometimes it is useful to be specific, particularly if you have specific needs related to what you want. When you're looking for a new home, your rep-resentation of the home you want should include all the details of what you want. Do you want to buy a house? Lease a condo? Rent an apartment? How many bedrooms and bathrooms? What price range? Do you want housemates? What areas do you want to live in? Anything that necessarily narrows your search should be represented in your magical symbol. A generalized symbol of lovely house for sale might turn up dozens of beautiful options thousands of miles from where you want to live, or cozy three room cottages for your urban family of six.

On the other hand, it's also important to include just enough space for unexpectedly positive results. In our house hunting example, when you're representing the areas you're searching in, you might want to include not just the neighborhoods you like most, but also any neighborhood with a commute you could handle, even if they're not your first choice. You might find that a house you never would have looked at otherwise just happens to have everything you want. Sometimes the things we think we want aren't always what we actually need, or something we think we don't want turns out to be better—or better for *us*—than we thought. To accommodate for this, some magicians will add a caveat to their sympathetic magic, representing what they want and including in their spell or energy work the sentiment "This, or whatever else would be better for me than this." Others place their magic under the oversight of a deity or spirit, generally one with whom they have an established relationship, and whom they trust to approve, veto, or guide their request.

Contagion is the idea that two objects that have been in contact continue to affect one another even after they have been separated. This bond is stronger the longer the two objects were in contact, and strongest when they were once a single object. The metaphysical concepts beneath contagion are first that physical matter has an energy body that wants to stay whole even after physical pieces have been separated, and second that two objects physically joined for long enough will begin to merge their energy.

The quintessential image of the witch using hair to cast a spell on someone is a common example of contagion. Hair has many of its own associations with a person's power, so it is both an obvious and common choice for people who want to easily direct their magic toward an individual. Of course, the most common examples are often ethically ambiguous at best, but that's a matter of the magician, not the tool. Used with consent from the subject of the spell, the power of contagion in a lock of hair can be an effective way to direct magic for healing, prosperity, or even love, if that's what the person in question wants.

Another common example of contagion is using a stone, shell or other natural object from a favorite place to connect with the energy of that place after you've gone. Intentionally refined and directed, these links can create effective power sources. For example, a smooth stone from someone's favorite beach can power a charm to help that person stay relaxed and calm even in tense situations. Not only do the physical characteristics of the rock itself help through the forces of similarity, but the stone also provides the person with a connection to the beach they love, letting them draw on the energy of that place to keep their calm.

When working with contagion in magic, remember that the connection goes both ways. You can access a person through bits of their hair, but they can also access you if you're in possession of their hair. The desire to act with consent should be motivation enough to behave ethically, but if it's not, know that having a lock of hair or drop of blood from someone does not give you mystical power over them, and many of us can effectively fight back through those same channels. Also be aware that if you're using an object connected to a place to power your magic, any changes in that place will also affect your spell. For this reason many people who work with semi-precious gemstones only use crystals sourced from mines that do not negatively impact the ecosystem, as they feel the connection to wounded land in other stones.

Paths of Power

Traditional Wicca teaches eight ways of raising, activating, or accessing different types of energy, often referred to as the eight paths of power. To my knowledge, the Wiccan eight paths first appear in Gardnerian lore in 1953, but it is entirely possible that they are older than that, as so much of Wicca was built from components far older than the system people practice today. Many other traditions, Wiccan and otherwise, have adopted and adapted these eight paths of power for their own use. Furthermore, the concept of an eightfold path (unrelated to these paths of power) appears in many traditions that significantly predate Traditional Wicca.

The general concept of the paths of power appealed to our group, although none of the lists of eight seemed quite right for us. There are many different ways of working magic and accessing energy, and there is great value in broadly approaching those paths of power as sources of insight. Furthermore, categorized modalities of magical practice are useful for training purposes, as they help both teacher and student assess their strengths and challenges. That said, we felt that the traditional eight paths were not quite as comprehensive as we'd like, and a few paths seemed unnecessarily specific. After reflecting on how we engage with magic and energy, we chose to expand both the quantity and definitions of the paths of power, resulting in the twelve categories we use now in Spectrum Gate Mysteries: Movement, Sound, Consumables, Divination, Meditation, Travel, Ritual, Ordeal, Energy, Connection, Creation, and Destruction. Our definitions for these categories are as follows:

❖ **Movement:** This path is about moving your physical body. Examples include dancing, martial arts, sports, jogging, and any other kinesthetic discipline. Physical exertion raises magical energy, and the path of movement teaches us embrace and utilize the power of our bodies.

❖ **Sound:** Music and rhythm have well documented affects on mind and body, and well-attested magical efficacy, but the path of sound doesn't just stop there. It also includes human speech, and the varied sounds of nature, from birdsong to crackling flames to waves crashing on the beach.

❖ **Consumables:** Shamans, magicians, and ritualists from traditions all over the world have an ancient history of consuming or administering various substances to access magical realms or heal the sick. The path of consumables covers these practices, but also includes using and making incense, as well as cooking. This last in particular we felt deserved a more prominent place in magical theory. Tremendous thought and energy can go into preparing a meal, and both cooking and sharing food can create powerful magic.

❖ **Divination:** From reading Tarot cards to interpreting omens to scrying in a black mirror, divination is how we peer at the webs of fate and chance, and seek insight from the Gods Themselves. Rather than a force to direct or harness, we gain through divination the subtle power of knowledge and insight.

❖ **Meditation:** If divination brings us insight from outside ourselves, meditation brings insight from within. From the inarticulate peace of the quiet mind to revelation earned through reflection, meditation helps us understand and connect with ourselves.

❖ **Travel:** At first travel may seem like it ought to be a subset of movement, but we felt the subtle differences are significant enough to warrant creating a separate category. On a physical level, movement is about moving your body within its own context, whereas travel is about changing that context altogether. Physical travel can be a tremendously spiritual experience, sometimes soothing, sometimes trying, but often enlightening. Changing context is an excellent way to shift out of old patterns, move stagnant energy, and find new perspective. On a spiritual level, the path of travel can also include astral projection, pathwalking, dream, and other types of journeying to mental and spiritual realms. On a metaphorical level, trying to see someone else's point of view is, in a sense, traveling to their perspective. Such a journey creates bonds between individuals that are most definitely sources of power.

❖ **Ritual:** It should come as no surprise that a book about group ritual includes ritual as a path of power. Remember, however, that rituals aren't just the circles you create with your coven, but also any magical or spiritual action that communicates something to yourself, to the Gods, or to your community. Greeting the newly waxing crescent moon with a witches' salute is a ritual, as is placing an offering at your devotional shrine. The path of ritual teaches us both how to create effective group ritual to share with others, and how to cultivate meaning in our own private acts of discipline and devotion.

❖ **Ordeal:** The path of ordeal is about seeking wisdom, insight, and empowerment through suffering. The most obvious examples are trials of pain or endurance through which one achieves catharsis, experiences a revelation, or finds themselves opened to or connected with some form of divinity. The ordeal path is actually much broader, however, including wide definitions of suffering, mental and emotional as well as physical, and the benefits to be reaped from it are limitless. Ordeal is not without its risks, however. Just as an otherwise beneficial substance can be lethal when prepared improperly or consumed in the wrong quantity, ordeal sought foolishly, or attempted without due care, can harm rather than help.

❖ **Energy:** Certainly all the paths of power are about raising or accessing energy, so having energy as its own path seems a bit confusing at first. The path of energy is perhaps the anti-path - it is the practice of sensing, directing, and manipulating energy with nothing more than one's own will. The fundamental principles of energy work described in the beginning of this chapter fall under the path of energy, as does the complex practice of drawing energy from a source, changing its fundamental nature, and shaping it into a metaphysical construct.

❖ **Connection:** Every relationships we create has power in it. Whether you're working with the love you share with a partner, an affinity for a specific object, or a sense of kinship within a community, those bonds can empower, strengthen, and stabilize. All of these, and more, fall within the path of connection.

❖ **Creation:** The path of creation includes any type of work that results in the physical manifestation of an item. Common crafts such as woodworking and knitting fall under creation, as would tending a garden. In a world where so much of what we have can be bought pre-made or manufactured by automated machines, it behooves us to reconnect with the power of physical reality by crafting some of our own ritual tools, or growing the food we offer in ritual. The time, energy, and effort required to make an object become a part of that object's power, and forge a connection between creator and creation.

❖ **Destruction:** From harvesting a crop to burning messages for the dead to cutting cords for releasing energy, destruction is just as much a source of power as creation. Food and drink offerings fall within this path, as do other sacrifices in which the item offered is destroyed.

Before we move on, we must make two important observations about the paths of power. First, the paths of power are not always exclusive. Many spiritual or magical activities involve a combination of paths of power. Yoga, for example, would be described by most as an act of both movement and meditation. Still other activities can involve many different paths of power depending on your intent and approach. Sex, for example, can be all about movement, or can be a combination of movement and connection, perhaps even adding creation or consumables. Categorizing the paths of power is not meant to limit the ways in which we engage with our activities, but to give us a framework within which to think about what we do. Rather than struggling to figure out which path of power an activity fits within, try to consider all possible paths of power it might reach, and how approaching the activity through those different lenses might add insight to your endeavor.

Finally, it is important to avoid narrow or ableist thinking as we approach working with the paths of power. While it may take some effort to find the best way, the truth is that everyone can engage with every path of power. Movement doesn't inherently require mobility, as we all have blood moving rapidly through our bodies; sound is at its heart simply vibrations, which can be felt and made in countless ways; what is ordeal for one person may be routine for another, and vice versa. What matters is that we all can and do hold power within ourselves. Some of paths of power will be more challenging, while others will come easily. This is true for everyone, and no one will master every path. Nevertheless, we have a responsibility, both to ourselves and to each other, to fully realize our potential, even as we remain ever conscious of our differences and our limitations.

Spellcraft

Spellcraft is where energy work, sympathetic magic, and the paths of power come together. A spell is a magical act performed with a specific goal, or a magical construct with a specific function. A spell can be as simple as wishing upon a star, or as elaborate as burning consecrated candles that have been oiled, engraved, and bound with charged and knotted cords, while the coven burns specially mixed incense and chants together in a circle dedicated to spirits and deities relevant to your intent. Some magicians find it useful to add as many correspondences and ritual acts as possible to reinforce the power of a spell, whereas others find that simple rituals allow them to better focus on pouring their energy into what they're doing. Most practitioners seem to fall somewhere in the middle, creating just enough ritual to put them in an appropriate headspace for magical working, but not so much as to distract them from their energy dynamics.

Today's Neopagan books are full of spells for almost any occasion. There is a certain draw to following someone else's spell, like cooking from a recipe; it evokes the image of the witch with her magical tome casting ingredients into a cauldron as she speaks a mystical incantation. Certainly there is power in tradition, so performing the same spell the same way as you or others have done many times before can lend extra momentum to you work. Furthermore, designing a spell requires time spent on careful planning; you might not always be able to create a new spell from scratch. However, the effort you put into designing your own customized spells adds power to your work that can't be replicated by flipping to a familiar page or scanning a table of contents. It's worth it to have both options available to you, so consider keeping a record both of the spells you design for yourself, and of other spells you find accessible and effective.

As this book's focus is Coven Craft, I won't get into the intricacies of solitary spellcraft. Instead, our purpose here is to investigate the use of magic in a coven. As discussed above, one of the biggest benefits of having a coven is being able to share your hopes and desires with a group of people who will help you achieve them. Revealing yourself in such a way creates vulnerability, and part of the point of a coven of established members sharing trust with one another is to have an environment in which you can do just that. Sometimes your entire coven might share a goal that you want to work on together, but if you have a personal need or desire, share that with your group too. They might be willing to help you achieve it, or at least support you in your own efforts.

If someone in your group proposes an act of spellcraft, consider what level of involvement you feel comfortable with. Would you cast the spell with them? Would you lend them your energy to help them cast the spell? Will you hold space for them to do their own work, but otherwise not participate personally? Do you not want to be involved at all? If you don't want to participate in casting the spell, could you offer the person resources to use on their own? Discuss your thoughts and feelings with your group, and remember that the person who asked for spellwork is putting themselves in a vulnerable position by asking for what they want. Treat them gently as you discuss their request, even if it's not something you want to participate in.

If your group declines to help you with a proposed spell, hear them out. Sometimes it's not a matter of moral objection, but rather a sense that some things should be done alone, or an issue of personal triggers or limits that have nothing to do with the spell itself being objectively good or bad. Sometimes the intensity of our desire makes something we would not otherwise consider seem completely reasonable. Presumably you trust your fellow coven members, so let them help you see the best in yourself, even if that's not who you feel in the moment.

The following questions can help guide you and your group through creating your own spells:

- ❖ What is your goal? Is it a goal shared by the group, or an individual's goal that the group supports?
- ❖ How does the group want to participate in the spell? Does everyone want to cast the spell together, or do some people want to provide energetic support while others perform the magical acts?
- ❖ Which paths of power does your group feel most comfortable with? Are any of them particularly appropriate for your goal?

❖ Are there any deities or spirits that you or other members of your group wish to work with in accomplishing your goal? If so, are They amenable to the task?

❖ What correspondences (e.g. stones, colors, herbs, astrological signs, etc.) are appropriate for your goal?

❖ Do you want to create a physical object to carry or anchor the energy of your spell outside of circle, or do you want to release power during circle and direct it to a specific affect?

❖ What will people do in circle to accomplish your goal? Will everyone perform the same act together? Will different people have different roles? Will one person perform a specific act while others direct energy towards it? What will those acts be?

❖ What materials are necessary to carry out your plan?

In essence, spells are tools, and as such have no inherent morality of their own. As a practitioner of ritual and magical arts, you must decide for yourself what your ethics are and how you must act on them. As a tradition that values education, free thought, and agency, our coven finds it unethical to subvert the thought, agency, and/or will of another person, but we also understand that absolutes are rare in real life. For example, I would not subvert another's will, unless their will was to do me harm, in which case I'd happily defend myself.

Every rule has exceptions. There is no easy guide that you can follow to ensure that you are an ethical person. You must think. You must consider what type of person you want to be, not just for others, but for yourself. We must not act solely out of impulse or strict adherence to a preset code. As practitioners of magic we forgo the luxury of ignorance and cultivate a constant awareness of how our actions affect everything around us.

Rites of Passage

A rite of passage marks a significant change in a person's life. These changes can be either interpersonal—affecting our relationships with other people—or intrapersonal—affecting our relationship with ourselves—or both. Cultures around the world have ways of observing these changes in both religious and secular ceremonies. In modern Paganism, special rituals can help us bring our spirituality to secular rites of passage, and let us mark momentous occasions that our culture might not otherwise recognize.

Any change that you or your group find significant can be honored with a rite of passage. Perhaps you feel a shift that you feel is important enough to warrant ceremonializing in circle, or maybe you are struggling with a change and think that a ritual might help you transition more easily. Talk to your group about what you need, and let them help you create a way to commemorate or ease whatever you're moving through.

What follows are a number of common general themes for rites of passage, along with various things to consider when approaching them. Our discussion here is in no way comprehensive, so don't think of this as an exhaustive guide. Rather let this be a starting point from which you and your group can explore social and personal transformation, what you might want to recognize in circle, and how you might want to go about it.

Birth

Birth is considered one of the original rites of passage, celebrated in some way or another by every human culture. The modern baby shower is a common secular observation of this impending social shift, and one that our Craft can easily adapt to suit our needs. For example, a coven could work magic intended to help expecting parents have a swift delivery of a healthy child.

We must not forget, however, that the social function of a baby shower has its own special power, particularly for Queer Pagans. Our society puts incredible pressure on parents to assign a gender to their child and teach them to conform through everything from apparel to pronouns. Parenting is already a challenging practice with so many competing theories on how children ought to be raised, and Queer parents will find that even more true. Whether they decide to go with a child's apparent sex until the child informs them otherwise, or not acknowledge any gender at all until the child chooses one, or take any other approach to their child's sex and gender, a coven can offer a priceless gift to Queer parents merely by supporting their choices in raising their children. There are various ways for a coven to demonstrate this support. Baby showers, blessing a nursery, birthing magic, and naming ceremonies are all opportunities for groups to give both magical and mundane aid to expecting parents.

If someone in your coven is expecting a child, ask them what, if anything, they would like to do to commemorate the occasion. Surprise parties can be fun for some people, but surprise magic presents ethical dilemmas and potential complications. Before sending energy to someone or working magic on their behalf, ask them what they want and what they don't want, and respect their wishes.

Wiccan couple Kathy and Adair wrote about the birthing of their child:

> When we had our first son, Thomas, our coven gathered with us a week later and we had a lovely Wiccaning ceremony, invoking the elements to protect and bless our baby, but the birthing itself took place in a hospital because Adair had a high-risk pregnancy. When Kathy chose to be the one to bear our second child, she was low-risk enough to have a home birth, and our son Carey was born with our coven-mates in the next room, drumming and chanting. We chose to have only the two of us and the midwife in the birthing room—someone else might be comfortable with giving birth in a big group of people, but Kathy was worried about clenching up at the last minute due to modesty issues, so they all gathered in the kitchen just outside and kept a series of songs and chants up for hours while she labored. A chosen friend popped in periodically to bring ice chips, extra pillows, and relieve Adair for bathroom and food breaks.
>
> We called them second, right after the midwife, when the labor started. Before things got seriously underway, they blessed the room and the bed, casting a circle and then quietly stepping out of it. We'd warned our coven-mates that the labor could go on for a day and a half—it's happened before, especially with first-time mothers—and that

they might want to be there in shifts. We warned them that something might go wrong and we'd have to relocate to the hospital—it was decided that in case of a hospital move they'd stay where they were and do ritual to send strength to mother and baby. We also warned them that there might be screaming, but not to take notice of it. (Adair cursed out the entire birthing crew minutes before giving birth—we took it as a sign that Thomas would have a feisty spirit!) It was wonderful to have our coven's support and to feel their presences, hear them singing and chanting, and know that our son would come into the world in a sacred circle.

Carey was born at sunset after about eight hours of labor. A cheer from the kitchen marked the sound of his first wail. As soon as the afterbirth passed and we got Kathy wiped down, hydrated, and covered with a quilt, we brought in our coven-mates and did the Wiccaning right there as he suckled at his mother's breast for the first time, and was then passed sleepily around in a bundle of blanket for individual blessings. It was a beautiful moment. Regardless of what spiritual path he chooses as an adult, he goes into this world with our gods and best wishes at his back.

Adoption

Many birth-related ceremonies focus on bringing a new person into a family. This important social and spiritual function applies not only to welcoming biological offspring, but also to adoption in various forms.

Some parents adopting an infant might choose to celebrate their adoption as if the child were their biological offspring. Using social and ritual observances identical to those expecting to give birth can help them and their community recognize that the child is no less "theirs" than if they'd birthed it themselves. Other parents might choose to create special adoption rituals as a way of magically establishing or formally recognizing the familial bond with their new baby. Adoption rituals for toddlers and older children can ease a transition into a new life for both parent and child, just as any rite of passage helps us conceptualize, process, and move through life's changes.

Welcoming a new member into a community can be seen as a form of adult adoption. Consider creating a coven joining ritual for your group as a way of formally recognizing when someone has made the shift between a frequent guest and a committed member. This will not only help the new member feel welcome, but also help the group strengthen their bonds with one another, and develop a sense communal identity.

Maturation

Maturation rituals, sometimes referred to as "coming of age" ceremonies, come in many forms, both secular and spiritual. Typically these rites of passage mark a person's transition from childhood to adulthood. One such physical transition which bears discussion is puberty.

Even for cisgendered people, puberty can be chaotic or even traumatic. For young Queer Pagans of any variety, maturation rites are fraught with difficulty; our culture constantly attempts to impose gender norms as we struggle to figure out who we are and who we want to be, all while our bodies shift in ways we usually can't control. Because puberty typically happens before the age of majority, rituals recognizing these physical changes will require the consent of that individual's parents or legal guardians.

I began my own journey into the Craft when I was a minor. I ached for a coven, but no one would even consider teaching me before I turned 18. It was a long, hard wait, and at the time, I didn't understand why someone wouldn't just help me. Eventually I designed a dedication ritual for myself, and to this day I am glad that I did. I created a ceremony that incorporated elements from dedication and initiation rites I'd read about in various books on Wicca and Paganism. Not only did this ritual help me make the mental, emotional, and spiritual shift I needed at the time, but when I experienced those incorporated elements again later in life as part of other initiation rites, it felt like a continuation of a path I'd started on my own. It is a hard thing to wait for a group and a community, but don't be afraid to create for yourself rites that will help you endure that period of solitude.

This can be a challenge, as many young Queer Pagans are not "out" with their family, but it is an unfortunate legal necessity. If you are a closeted Queer Pagan looking to mark your journey through your body's changes with rites of passage, consider creating your own solitary rites of passage. Reflect on who you are and who you want to become, and design a ritual that represents your ideal transformation.

As adults it is easy to imagine the maturation rite we wish we'd had, and assume that the young members of our community would want the same, but we must remember that we are all individuals with different needs and desires. What worked or might have worked for you could be horrifying to someone else. If a member of your group or a child of one of your members is undergoing puberty, let them decide if they want a maturation rite at all. If they do, let them choose which physical changes they do and don't want to recognize, and let them determine the significance of those changes. Give them space to discuss their thoughts and feelings with their parent or parents without pressure in any direction. If they do choose to have a rite of passage, create a ritual that honors the specific shifts that are meaningful to them, and confirms their emerging sense of adult identity.

Of course, physical changes are far from the only sign of adulthood, and the mental, emotional, and spiritual ways we mature are just as important as physical development. Many different occasions can be hallmarks of maturation for different people. Learning to drive a car, getting a first job, completing school, moving out to live on your own, having sex, or even filing your own taxes for the first time can all feel like defining moments of developing maturity. All of these can be commemorated with ritual to become a rite of passage.

Moving

Moving from one home to another is very obviously an event of physical passage, but also involves mental, emotional and spiritual transition. The process of finding a new home, packing up, leaving or even selling an old home, and settling into a new home is exhausting even when everything goes smoothly (rare as that is). Rites of passage help us recognize the value of the home we are leaving behind and say goodbye to the life we lived there. Home cleansing and blessing rituals can leave an old home hospitable to whoever lives in it next, and create a comfortable environment in a new home. Permanent wards around a new home offer constant protection, and can help energy-sensitive residents find sanctuary from the energetic static of daily life.

A very simple blessing technique involves carefully choosing which items are first brought into a new home—bringing in money ensures prosperity, roses can work for love, food for sustenance, salt for protection, and so forth. Sometimes items are brought into the home individually with some explanation of their significance; some people put everything into a basket or other container and treat the entire collection as a magical talisman. Whatever route you choose, consider your personal connection to the items you select as well as traditional associations. It's your home, so consecrate it your way.

Many Neopagans find that their home has a permeating energy that manifests as some type of spirit. This spirit is not always aware or even anthropomorphic, and it can be as complex as an entity that seems to have agency and communicates with its inhabitants, or simple as an animistic sense of presence within the building itself. When you create your rites of passage for a move, consider adding gestures of farewell to the spirit of an old home, and a greeting to the spirit of a new home. Awareness of and respect for the land we live on should include man-made structures as well as natural features.

Transition

A book about ritual specifically designed to be inclusive of Trans people must include rites of passage for transition. I, however, not being Trans, cannot write this section alone. I can offer suggestions as a ritual designer, but I will not pretend to know what a Trans person's experience is like, or what they might want from a rite of passage. Instead I have asked a few people who identify as Trans in various ways to share their thoughts on the subject.

Kailin, one of our founding coven members, wanted a ritual to provide structure for the process of intense introspection surrounding their transition. They write:

Sometime before my top surgery a year ago, Spectrum did a ritual to help me prepare for the procedure. Prior to the ritual I did a lot of meditation and thinking about what was to come. Even through the ritual and my reflections prior and post, what I learned did not come to me until much later. When I finally figured it out, I realized that top surgery may not be the final answer in my transition and, in fact, it created more questions. In the moment the ritual was intense and was hard to hear and accept. In truth, I was definitely uncertain, but that uncertainty did not change my decision to go through with the procedure. I wonder sometimes, had I not had that opportunity for reflection within Spectrum, would I have felt more incomplete post surgery than I do now? My transition is far from complete; I know that now and can continue to grow from here.

Sometimes rituals can be unexpectedly challenging. When difficult revelations or messages arise, support shouldn't stop when the circle is dispersed. The aid we offered Kailin didn't end with their ritual. One of our members helped them get to and from the hospital for appointments, and spent time with them while they were healing. We all offered moral support, and helped Kailin process their experiences constructively. Sometimes that meant talking frankly about what was happening, and sometimes that just meant showing them they were a welcome and important member of our community exactly as they were in that moment.

Not everyone will want a formal rite of passage to commemorate their transition. Owen Tashlin writes:

As someone who is not naturally drawn to formal ritual as an expression of personal growth, I have struggled a great deal with the topic of rites of passage for some time. Not having any of the traditional touchstones of growing up male in our society (be that a good or a bad thing) I have had to construct for myself much of what it means for me to no longer identify as female and move into my fully-fledged male identity. While it is tempting to point to medical milestones as the obvious choice in my own journey, that tends to push the scale to the side of favoring the physical experience of gender rather than the emotional or spiritual facets that can often be neglected.

> *A rite of passage for me is a marker in time, a delineation between one state and the next. For myself, I would say that I relate to the everyday actions that I experience as a constant rite that I am working through. It is a rite of passage every time I either assert or correct pronoun usage, rather than simply ignore or brush off misgendering as something to be endured in exchange for the familiar discomfort of being in the closet in my professional life. Every time I push through my own natural inertia and disrupt my own status quo, I am pushing into an unknown and looking for ways to mark that change for next time so that I can look back and see how far I have come. That said, these smaller events are easy to lose track of in the shuffle of day to day life. It's a dilemma that I haven't truly come a decision about, though no doubt that in itself will be a kind of rite as well.*

If someone in your group dislikes the idea of a formal rite of passage or transition ritual, consider supporting them outside of circle instead. Something as seemingly simple as helping others remember and use the person's correct pronouns can show affirmation of both social and spiritual identity. Ask the person what type of support they want from their coven in acknowledging their transition. Respect their right to choose this for themselves, as that in and of itself is an act of support.

If one of your members does want a rite of passage, but wants one that focuses on emotional and spiritual identity rather than physical experience, consider a ritual that intentionally uses appropriate gendered language as much as possible. Ask the person what pronouns and titles they want for themselves, and what other social and spiritual elements they want to include in their presentation. Design a ritual that heaps these personal markers on them, highlighting and celebrating their identity. Rituals such as these may be a good time to intentionally embrace gendered terms like "priest" or "priestess" if that is desirable, helpful, and appropriate for the person in question.

For more examples of transition rituals, check out the book *Hermaphrodeities: The Transgender Spirituality Workbook* (Raven Kaldera, Asphodel Press 2008).

Marriage

Our most common marriage rites can include bridal and groom showers, bachelor and bachelorette parties, and, of course, wedding ceremonies. Most people getting married have specific ideas for what type of wedding ritual they want. A coven should offer support in whatever ways the engaged individuals might want it. While some people choose to get married in circle by officiators from their coven, many don't. Wedding design and officiation is its own ritual specialty, and there are a number of prenuptial concerns to address which are beyond the scope of this book.

Showers and parties, however, can be wonderful opportunities for a coven to give extra love, support, and magic to an upcoming wedding or a recent union. Talk to the people getting married about what they would find helpful or welcome. For example, do they want a ritual for long term stability, or fertility magic for future children, or a celebration to highlight their magical ties within the web of your community? Find out what social or spiritual changes they want to honor in ritual, and design a rite that suits their needs within the context of your group.

For more information on Pagan wedding rituals, including advice for Pagan clergy, you can check out *Handfastings and Wedding Rituals: Welcoming Hera's Blessing* (Raven Kaldera, Llewellyn Press, 2003).

Divorce

Divorce rarely gets the ritual attention alloted to marriage, yet its affect on a person's life is just as profound. Sometimes a divorce is so difficult that the person wants to hold their sorrow in solitude, which makes it a matter of personal observance rather than group ritual. Sometimes the people getting divorced must attend to their diverging paths on their own, again precluding coven involvement. For those who wish it, however, divorce rituals can help people amicably part ways, find closure through ritualized observance of their change in status, or magically cut ties from a toxic relationship (this last in particular is useful for addressing any sort of harmful relationship, not just marriages). As with every other rite of passage, talk to the person or people involved, and let them guide the design process.

Ritual is far from the only way that a coven can support people going through divorce. Just being present as a source of non-judgmental support is an incredible gift. When I split up with my ex-husband, I was shocked by how degraded I felt in the eyes of everyone from my parents to my cable provider. Changing my name after my wedding had been so easy, but getting my old name back was an uphill battle in every direction. The Wiccan coven I was a member of at the time was there for me through all of it. In circle with them I felt just as welcome as ever. I was not a failure because I couldn't keep a marriage together; I was a success because I recognized my own limits and pursued the life I wanted for myself. My teacher helped me establish and maintain self-care habits, and my group showed me a spiritual community that had my back. All this didn't come in the form of a special ritual, but it was most definitely a rite of passage, and part of our Coven Craft.

Career

Significant career changes can be another modern rite of passage. Ritual commemoration of an important new job or career shift help us bring our spirituality into our work, and see the mundane work we do as extensions of our spiritual selves. For some, this connection is obvious. The devotee of Njord who works as an oceanographer, or the servant of Aphrodite who works as a sex educator, can easily see how their jobs relate to their spirituality. For others, however, sacredness might be found not specifically in what their work is, but in the fact that they support themselves or their family. For people who must endure a job they dislike, rituals honoring their effort can provide spiritual sustenance to help them cope. A little thank you can go a long way; ceremonial gratitude can go even further.

"Career" does not have to mean holding a steady job, or doing any sort of paid work at all. Taking a broader and more inclusive approach to career means acknowledging all the ways in which individuals contribute to their families or their communities. Whatever you do with your life, however you participate in the world around you, that is your career. The completion of an elaborate art series is just as worth recognition as a successful home improvement project or a high profile promotion. Whatever you determine to be a significant point in your career can be honored with a rite of passage, and a supportive coven will join you in celebrating your achievements.

Elevations

Elevation rituals are rites of passage that serve multiple functions. As a teaching and training tool, they can help structure spiritual education and provide community recognition of a student's progress. Because elevations typically come with requirements that must be fulfilled or achieved before each rank, they give structure to spiritual training. The more rigorous or challenging the training, the more helpful it is for the student to have clear goals and benchmarks to focus on; rather than looking at the entirety of the curriculum (which can be quite overwhelming) the student need only look to the next step, and what must be accomplished between here and there.

Of course, elevations also serve a spiritual function. Initiations of various types exist in cultures from around the world, and they have in common an element of Mystery. "Mystery" is capitalized here because we're not just talking about the rites being kept secret, although this is sometimes the case as well; Mystery in this context refers to something that defies articulation. Someone could try to tell you what an initiation is like, but the reality is profoundly more than its description. Words often cheapen the experience, and expectation in someone who's heard what an initiation is "supposed" to be like or "supposed" to mean can spoil the entire affair. I suspect that this is a large part of why so many initiation rituals are kept secret; if you don't know what's coming, you have no choice but to be fully present in that moment, processing things as they happen and allowing for whatever significance they take in the context of that sacred instant.

The ranks and elevations we use in our coven are described in the chapter starting on page 148. Our approach is obviously inspired by traditional Wicca, but we modified it in ways and for reasons I shall discuss there.

Death

Death is another of humanity's original rites of passage, with our oldest burial customs dating back to the Paleolithic age. Neopagan rituals around death and dying tend to focus on easing a person's transition into whatever awaits them beyond life, and as such are uniquely customized to that person's beliefs. Rituals for the terminally ill can help people spiritually prepare for death through both community support and spiritual context. Funerals help ease the transition of the soul, and help loved ones express and process their grief. Memorial rituals help us carry the burden of loss, and sustain our relationships with beloved dead and ancestors alike.

My father's passing hit me like a truck. He had been diagnosed with cancer almost ten years prior, and our family had finally gotten to a point where chemo treatments and side effects started to seem normal. One evening we all had dinner together—my mother, sister, father and I. Joking and laughing, we planned a family vacation for later that summer. It was a rare thing for the four of us to be together and all get along. The next day was my birthday, and my sister and I went out to celebrate. That night my mother called to tell us he was dying. A week later, he was gone.

For months after he died, I was a wreck. I was fortunate enough to have had a good relationship with a supportive and loving father, but my family was far from idyllic, and he had often been my foundation and my shelter. At the time of his passing, I was a second-degree initiate in a traditional Wiccan coven. I was supposed to be leading the group as part of my training for third degree, but in my cloud of grief and unreasonable expectations of myself, I didn't think to ask for any help. Perhaps ritual grieving would have eased the emotional burden I carried, or helped repair my relationship with Haides, the Greek God of the Dead, which took me more than a year to resolve on my own. Instead, for three months I lived in a computer game, told everyone I was fine, and had flashbacks of touching his empty body every time I closed my eyes.

Just after I'd turned twenty I had come out to my father as Pagan, polyamorous, and bisexual. He'd accepted the first two, although he asked me not to reveal them to the rest of my family, but he could not accept my sexual orientation. He never wanted to meet or even hear about any of my girlfriends. It was the only part of my life and my identity that he utterly rejected.

By the Samhain after he passed, I knew I needed to face my father's death in sacred space. I needed to part the Veil between worlds, welcome him into circle, and accept that he was now amongst the dead. Weekly therapy had me in a better mental and emotional place than in the months before, but I was still afraid of welcoming my very Catholic father into a Wiccan circle. Would he, as one of the Beloved Dead, be able to see more of me than he could in life? And what would he think of what he saw? Even then, traditional though my coven was, most of us were Queer in some way, and we enjoyed being a group that bucked convention. Could I face my father with all of the parts of myself that I'd hidden from him in life? Would he be more accepting of me in death?

Four of us went out into the woods to cast a circle and part the Veil. It was a simplified ritual, with focus on acknowledging our ancestors. The three people who accompanied me were my teacher, with whom I'd studied for six years at that time, and two covenmates with whom I had been worshipping since I joined my teacher's coven. Ostensibly the ritual was for all of us, but everyone knew what I was facing, and they quietly supported me. The trust I shared with them let me be vulnerable enough to call out his name across the Veil, yet strong enough to welcome him when he came. It certainly didn't heal everything, but ritually accepting his death allowed me to start forming a healthy relationship with his passing, and for the first time since I felt his spirit depart life, I knew that my father was dead, but not gone. That too was a relief.

As members of our community age and die, we are faced with our own mortality, and begin to consider what arrangements we must make, both to prepare for our own journey, and to protect our loved ones and chosen family. When Keith, a beloved elder of Blue Star Wicca, was diagnosed with late-stage pancreatic cancer, he took immediate steps to ensure that his death would be handled according to his wishes. As a Gay Pagan priest, he was not well accepted by his family. He wanted to be honored with a Pagan funeral, so he created an advance health care directive, designating two other elders in his tradition—Cat and Vicki—as his health care proxies. He also gave Vicki power of attorney, and made her the executor of his estate. Cat and Vicki were accompanied by a third elder, Sabrina, who supported both them and Keith with every step along the way. These ladies were kind enough to share their story with me.

Keith's advance health care directive included a dispensation of body clause, which might have covered any legal considerations for his funeral rites, but no one challenged Cat, Vicki or Sabrina as they carried out Keith's wishes. While Keith was very openly gay, he was a Pagan priest first, and a gay man second. He wanted to be honored in death as a priest who had served his Gods in life, so his sexual orientation did not significantly affect his funeral rites.

As we campaign for social justice and advocate for free and open expression of every identity, we must remember to let other people choose what they want to express of themselves, and how they want to express it. Keith's Queerness was tremendously relevant to many of the people who knew and studied Witchcraft under him, but his funeral was about respecting his wishes, not theirs, which is as it should be. Just because someone may be Queer or Trans does not mean that we can assume they want that identity to be a focus in their funeral. Sometimes they will, and sometimes they won't. Let them speak for who they are, and how they want to be remembered.

Keith, Vicki, Cat, and Sabrina were lucky to have had their paperwork in order, and to proceed with Keith's beautiful funeral ceremony without conflict from Keith's family. They were also fortunate to have had many other members of their tradition and greater Pagan community offering their support. However, even in these nearly ideal circumstances, there was one place where Vicki and Sabrina ran into trouble.

Keith wanted to be an organ donor, and after he passed Vicki was contacted by an organization that wanted to harvest his corneas. The representative she spoke to aggressively pushed for contact with Keith's biological or legal family, as she and Sabrina did not have a dispensation of body form. Each state has its own regulations and its own form regarding the dispensation of a body. While the aforementioned clause in the advanced healthcare directive might have been enough to win a legal battle, this was far from Vicki's mind as she struggled with the combative representative despite her own grief from losing a loved one. Seeing that Vicki was at her wits end, Sabrina took the phone and firmly explained that as a gay man, Keith did not want his disapproving family having anything to do with his death.

As soon as Sabrina said the word "gay", the representative's tone changed. Suddenly, after all the harassment they'd put Vicki though, they no longer wanted Keith's corneas, just because he was gay. Vicki was rightfully enraged, and to this day the moment stands out to her as an infuriating insult to Keith, to his generosity, and to gay men everywhere.

Vicki's advice to Queer Pagans is to look up your state's regulations regarding the dispensation of a body, and make sure that you have all the necessary forms filled out according to law (typically these forms must not only be signed, but witnessed and notarized as well). While gay men are not prohibited from being organ donors in the United States, they can still face prejudice from individuals, hospitals, and organizations if their sexual orientation is known. Learn what your options are, and what legal recourse you and your loved ones will have should any problems arise.

As far as other practicalities go, Raven Kaldera, a minister in a congregational-model legal Pagan church that has many GLBTQ parishioners, sent this advice on Pagan funeral planning to us for the book:

Pagans might have many reasons why leaving funeral plans to one's blood kin isn't the best option. Especially in states where the next-of-kin have overriding rights, it can help for one's Pagan group to create an official funeral plan to fill out—perhaps one that does not specify religion, but simply denotes that this is the religious group of which Person X is a committed member—and send it to one's relatives. Generally, all but the most possessive or vengeful family members will be relieved that in the case of Person X's death, all details will be handled by an established group, and all they have to do is to show up and mourn. These plans are useful and important not only for LGBTQ members who many not have supportive family, but also Pagans who want a Pagan funeral and know that their next-of-kin won't give it to them, and also members who have no next-of-kin (a problem for some who are aging and don't have children or surviving partners). Some of the points that a funeral plan should cover are:

❖ Who is the executor of the will and estate? (This can be a member of the Pagan group, but if it isn't, the executor needs to be kept in the loop about the plan, and shouldn't have any reservations about it. Choose carefully.) Where is the will kept? Give out multiple copies, including one that goes to an attorney to keep.

❖ What do they want done with their body? Cremation costs money—a funeral plan should include a cremation fund, accessible to the executor upon the death of the individual, or if they are destitute and there is a low-cost cremation option in your state, the paperwork means to prove this quickly. On the other hand, as expensive as cremation might be, traditional funeral home embalming, coffining, and burial is usually ten times as expensive, and harder on the environment. Cremains can be buried almost anywhere; whole bodies are more difficult. Some states have options for ecological green burial, but this needs to be checked out beforehand.

❖ A plain (or highly decorated) wooden casket can be made before death, or just afterwards by the Pagan group if they have the means to do so; it can be a ritual project, a way of preparing everyone for the oncoming death of a loved one, a way of mourning together that pours out emotion as creativity, and a way of honoring them. Even if it's going to go up in flames, it can be carved with messages to the Gods, and "grave goods" can be put in with the body—things they would have loved in life. (Make sure these are safe to burn or bury.)

❖ Some Pagans, being more ecologically minded, are pushing back against the toxic chemical processes used in modern embalming, and would prefer to go back to the era where loved ones cleaned the body and set up a home funeral, and then sent the body on to be burned or decay naturally in the earth. If this is something the individual wants, the Pagan groups needs to get trained in the simple safety procedures of home funerals. Classes in home funerals are sometimes taught by local hospice organizations (our group took one such course), or you can contact the National Home Funeral Alliance at www.homefuneralalliance.org for more information. A home funeral usually protects the body with a bed of dry ice. Cleaning and preparing the body can be seen as a service to the Gods of Death. The Pagan group should have copies of the paperwork necessary to move the body from one location to the next, perhaps pre-signed by the executor, spouse, or next-of-kin.

❖ Are organs to be harvested? If so the organization to whom they are left should be contacted, and potential issues ironed out beforehand.

❖ What kind of a funeral do they want? Points to consider might be what deities to invoke. what songs to sing, and what ritual actions to take. Decide if the funeral should even be openly and obviously Pagan; if there will likely be non-Pagan relatives attending, the individual might want "Pagan Lite" service, with subtle allusions rather than blatant ritual. Remember that it's up to the person in question, not the rest of the group. Do they want two rituals—a more generic one for all comers and a special one just for their Pagan group members?

❖ What beliefs does the individual hold about where they will go after death? Make sure to keep this in mind for the funeral rite—it's rude to insert prayers later that wish their soul to go someplace they didn't want to go.

❖ What do they want to wear, and/or have laid next to them for the ritual? Do they want anything burned or buried with them? (One Pagan went into the cremation fire with his wooden rune set; another went in with her wooden staff.) Do they want a giveaway, with some of their possessions given freely to the people at the funeral, or to specific people beforehand? Which possessions?

❖ Is the group expected to provide a reception with refreshments? Will there be a time for "telling of the tales" about that person?

❖ If their legal name is not the name they want spoken, carved on a stone, or otherwise referred to at their funeral, how will the group go about making sure of this? Preferred pronouns may also be an issue, especially with attendees who haven't seen the individual in a long time. Is there a kind and sensitive way to announce this at

the beginning of the ritual, or take people aside and brief them
gently in a way that takes their grief into consideration?

❖ Is there anyone they *don't* want allowed at the funeral, for whatever reason? (Some people, unfortunately, might come in order to
disrupt things; it's happened, especially with the funerals of
LGBTQ individuals.) How will the Pagan group enforce this wish?

❖ Do they want a memorial of some kind? Will funds be provided
for this, and by whom?

❖ How will news of their death and funeral be spread?

For information on Pagan funeral rites, see *The Pagan Book of Living
and Dying: Practical Rituals, Prayers, Blessings, and Meditations on Crossing
Over* by Starhawk and M. Macha Nightmare, HarperOne 1997.

Covens

Creating A Coven

Perhaps you are lucky enough to live in an area with an established coven. Most groups that are open to new members will advertise online, either through a site like *The Witches' Voice* (www.witchvox.com), or through social media. Maybe you'll find a coven with a practice that affirms a spectrum of gender, sex, orientation, and identity, or maybe you'll find a coven willing to adapt what they do for inclusivity.

Unfortunately, covens in general are currently in short supply, and Queer-affirming covens even more so (Queer-*friendly* covens are actually quite common, but most perpetuate the binary language and ritual practices found in Wicca, which is why I consider them Queer-*friendly*, but not queer-*affirming*). Many seekers are unable to find a local group, and their desire for a spiritual community leads them to creating one. If you find yourself in this position, before you do anything else, ask yourself a few questions.

First of all, what do you want to get out of being in a coven? Do you want ritual practice? Spiritual support? A community to celebrate holidays with? Are you looking for a short-term group that will study together for a while and then go their separate ways, or a long-term group that will establish enduring bonds with one another? Do you want a group that focuses on training and education, or a group that focuses on working together towards common goals? Do you want a group with intense focus, or something comfortably casual? How often would you want to meet, and would you want to cast a circle at every meeting, or have some purely educational or social gatherings as well? Everyone will have some things they do want, some things they don't want, and a few that could go either way. Keep a mental list of what you're looking for and what you want to avoid, and when you're ready, look for people with similar needs, goals, and limits.

Of course, finding people is easier said than done. These days the best place to find people for just about any special interest is the internet. Apps, forums, and social media sites have us more connected than we've ever been. The internet changes so rapidly, however, that I hesitate to include a comprehensive guide to online networking; what's popular now could be entirely obsolete within just a few years. Thankfully it's getting easier and easier to navigate the virtual world. Whatever the latest apps or best new sites happen to be, I suspect a basic web search can point you in the right direction.

If online networking doesn't suit you, other options do exist, although they will be much easier in a city or suburb. Some Neopagan or spiritual shops will host open classes or discussion groups, and people seeking a coven often attend. Sometimes an entirely mundane shared interest can lead to discussions of spirituality, which in turn lead to the beginnings of a group. Our coven's founding members met through a shared interest in kink, and established our earliest connections through conversations about the interplay between sexuality and spirituality.

Once you've met some people with whom you think you might want to start a group, there are a few things you should disclose right off the bat. The list of needs, limits, and goals is a good place to start. By this point you've probably already hit on many of those items, but go through them all again anyway, and be thorough. You don't want to find out after a year of intense emotional and spiritual investment in a coven that, while you were looking for a long-term spiritual community, someone else just wanted an transient practice group. Remember that there's no right or wrong thing to want or need. Everyone's desires are equally legitimate, even if they're not always compatible, and it's better to figure out any incompatibilities earlier rather than later.

If you think you might end up teaching other coven members, you should be very clear from the outset about your own level of experience and education. Whether you plan to be the organizer for a study group that learns ritual and magic together, a teacher for a student with a formal apprenticeship, or anything in between, make sure that the other people involved have a accurate understanding of your background.

Similarly, if you think you might end up as the group leader, make sure the other members know whether or not you've had any experience in that role. There is no specific amount of education or training you must have in order to run a group (although most traditional Wiccans will assert that a group is not truly a coven without at least one initiate, and some require that the initiate be of the third degree). People run groups out of necessity all the time, and more than a few traditional Wiccan covens began as eclectic study groups while one or more members pursued their initiation. Do whatever you feel must be done, but do it honestly.

If you end up organizing a coven for more than a year or so, you'll eventually be faced with a difficult decision: will you allow teens to join your group? As mentioned above, there are important legal considerations for the involvement of minors. Some groups will allow teens or children to be present as long as they are accompanied by a parent or legal guardian. Some groups will allow teens to participate with explicit parental consent. Most groups, however, avoid the issue altogether, and require that all members be at least eighteen years of age. There is no right answer here. Many teenagers, especially Queer teens, desperately need spiritual support as they are figuring out who they are and how they fit into the world. For these individuals, a coven willing to work with them is invaluable. That said, the potential dangers from an angry parent are very real, even when a group requires a guardian be present, or obtains explicit consent. We can make sure to act within the law, and take steps to protect each other, but even when we do everything right, there is still risk. Thus, each coven must make its own decision about how to proceed, and these decisions often need to be made on a case-by-case basis.

Coven Dynamics

Once you've gathered a group of people with common goals, you'll need to figure out how you want your coven to operate. The first thing you'll want to decide is what sort of leadership structure to arrange.

Some covens stick with a single leader who has final say on everything. Groups that function successfully with this sort of leadership intentionally develop communication and mutual understanding amongst their members, and trust that the person in charge will make decisions in the best interest of the group. One benefit of this type of leader is an excellent ability to get things done. A strong and authoritative leader can make decisions quickly, and let the group focus more on doing than on deciding what to do. On the other hand, not everyone is right for this type of leadership, either as the leader or as one of the members. Group leaders who act without considering the needs and desires of their group, but simply wield authority because they can, swiftly earn the ire of their members. Coveners who feel trapped under a leader who never acknowledges them will be understandably upset, and are likely to leave the group. If you choose to have a single leader in charge of your group, urge that leader to contemplate the difference between authoritative and authoritarian action, and have your leader regularly check in with every member to hear their wants and their frustrations.

Some covens have one leader in charge at a time, but periodically change who that is. Typically these leaders run the group for a predefined amount of time, with some groups letting them keep the leadership for another term if they choose, and others requiring that leadership changes hands at the end of every term. Rotating leadership in this way is an excellent way to ensure that no one burns out from constantly having to be in charge, and assures group members that they too can have a turn at the wheel if they are not entirely satisfied with the way the group is going.

However, this can sometimes lead to a sort of competition for who can lead the best, causing more tension than it eases. Additionally, if everyone is required to take a turn leading the group periodically, then eventually someone who does not want to lead or is not well suited to lead will end up in charge of the group, to the detriment of all. If you choose to pass leadership amongst your members, consider letting individuals choose whether or not they want to accept that role, and encourage everyone to communicate with each other just as they would if they had one permanent leader, rather than silently biding their time until they get to force their way.

Some covens run like a democracy, with members voting on every decision. This can be an excellent way to let everyone feel that they participate in deciding their group's path, but it can also get complicated and cumbersome. When does a new person get the right to vote on decisions relating to the group? If four new students join a group of three people who have spent years working together, would they suddenly be able to overturn decisions made by the others? Would your group appreciate the fresh perspective and new direction that would bring, or would the longstanding members feel that the coven they created was being taken from them? Which decisions necessitate a vote at all? Will you vote on the goal for every ritual? Will you vote on who brings what type of food for your post-ritual feast? Or will you have a coven charter that describes the general operation of your group, and only vote on what goes on it, or any changes made to it? If you choose to have a democratic coven, think about the practicalities of voting, and consider creating a structure that can handle logistical minutia, saving votes for more important decisions.

Some covens are run by consensus. Any time a decision needs to be made, the entire group discusses the issue together until everyone agrees on a course of action. Rule by consensus allows everyone an opportunity to influence the course of their group, but that opportunity is not always equal. Some people are naturally more outspoken than others; loud speakers and forceful personalities can drown out quieter individuals, and discussions aimed at finding consensus can be downright dreadful for extreme introverts. Some members might just keep arguing until everyone who disagrees just gives in so that the conversation can be over. Even the best consensus-run covens can take a dismayingly long time to reach a decision, particularly when compared to a coven run by an authoritative leader. If you choose to run your group by consensus, find ways to ensure that softer personalities get an equal voice to their louder counterparts. You may want to appoint a moderator to ensure that conversations stay on topic, and everyone gets a turn to speak. Consider letting members write down their thoughts ahead of time if they have trouble speaking up on the spot, or if they're unable to be present for an important debate.

Coven roles don't have to stop with the leader. In fact, creating different jobs for each covener can be an excellent way for a group to show their appreciation for the various contributions of its members. In *Wicca Covens* (1999), Judy Harrow discusses the benefit of creating as many coven roles as people want to fill, and describes a number of examples. Some of the coven roles we have considered include:

❖ **Scheduler:** Being a group leader is a big job all by itself, and trying to schedule times for circle can be excruciatingly complicated with a large or busy group. We decided to lessen the leader's workload by giving scheduling responsibilities to someone else, and decided that scheduling was hard enough that it could be its own coven role.

❖ **Food Coordinator:** Large ritual feasts, particularly when food allergies, taboos, or guests are involved, can be logistically complicated. Groups that often include elaborate banquets or pot-luck dinners find it helpful to have a food coordinator whose sole responsibility is to make sure that everyone can have enough to eat during celebratory meals (no more wheat pasta dinners for people with gluten allergies, or pot-lucks featuring a light salad and six desserts).

❖ **Scribe:** Many covens find it useful to keep records of when they meet, what they do, and how it went. This allows everyone to look back on their progress as a group, and identify any patterns that either need avoiding or are worth enhancing. A scribe can be responsible for keeping such a record, as well as for taking notes at any meetings or debates concerning coven operations.

❖ **Teacher:** Training students is an intense responsibility. Teachers are often also the best qualified to lead a group, but we would like to see these roles divided whenever possible. Without also having to coordinate daily operations and logistics as leaders, coven teachers would be able to focus entirely on creating the best possible curriculum and support structures for their students. While this goal may yet be a ways off for us, it is a dream we continue to strive for.

Teaching and Training

Coven Craft will inevitably include some sort of education. That education can take the shape of coveners learning from one another as they study the Craft and practice together, formally studying with a qualified teacher using planned lessons and training exercises, or anything in between. Good teachers can be frustratingly hard to find, so it's important for all of us to support the ways in which people can learn and develop their skills independently. Nevertheless, it's worth taking a moment to examine the benefits of training with a teacher.

A well-rounded Coven Craft teaching curriculum includes three broad categories of education: content knowledge, skill training, and spiritual mentorship. These categories are not mutually exclusive—often activities or assignments will include elements of each—but they are convenient ways for us to conceptualize and examine the education offered by a teacher, and how it differs from independent learning.

Content knowledge is the easiest category to approach independently. This category includes all of the ideas and theories we learn about ritual, magic, spirituality, energy, and religion, as well as mythology, magical correspondences, lore, and just about anything else that's declarative, or capable of being written down. This content can most definitely be absorbed through reading books—it is what you, dear reader, are accumulating right now. A seeker does not necessarily need a teacher in order to gather content knowledge. A teacher can help their student learn content by presenting it in different ways to accommodate their specific learning styles, but some independent learners are capable of providing this for themselves. Teachers can aid this process, but they aren't strictly necessary.

Skills include anything you actively do, from grinding resin to just the right consistency for the type of incense you want to make, to directing energy into a sphere to create a magic circle. While these skills can be learned through trial and error, or practicing exercises you read in books, a teacher can demonstrate a skill, analyze your technique, and give pointers catered to how you learn and exactly what you need to do to strengthen your ability. Many self-taught ritualists and magicians develop impressive skills on their own, so it's certainly possible to cultivate your own abilities, but a teacher can make the learning process a easer, and can help you progress faster. Teachers can also offer techniques that can't be easily described or put into words, and some will keep a few personal tricks of their trade that they only pass on to their students.

Spiritual mentorship simply can't be found in a book. Books can teach you about mentorship, and Judy Harrow's *Spiritual Mentoring* (2002) is an excellent resource to that effect. A mentor, however, must be a person. Mentors nourish you through the learning process. They help you understand yourself and your needs, and support you through the challenges and rigors of your training. They believe in you when you don't believe in yourself, and inspire you to be more and better than you were, and to be only and all that you are. A seeker can learn the Craft without a mentor, but the inarticulable benefits gained from mentorship cannot be gotten any other way.

Finding a Teacher

There are plenty of good reasons to seek a Craft teacher, but finding one who's right for you is easier said than done. If you decide you want to train with someone, the following questions can help guide your search:

❖ What exactly do you want to learn? Make a list of all the things you want your education to include, and find someone who can teach you those specific things.

❖ What are your strongest learning styles? Exceptional educators will be able to help you figure out how you learn best, but most Pagan teachers lack a background in pedagogy, and will need you to help them understand how to help you. Spend some time thinking about what kinds of assignments and activities would be most helpful for you, and what would just be boring, off-putting, or more challenging in method than in substance. Ask a potential teacher how they like to teach. Do they lecture? Give written assignments? Participate in learning exercises with their students? Reflect on whether or not those methods are likely to be helpful to you.

❖ How do you want your education to be structured? Do you want a casual arrangement with someone you can learn from, or a formal student-teacher agreement? How often do you want to communicate with your teacher? How frequently do you want to have lessons? What type of workload are you willing and able to take on? Do you want your training to include elevations?

❖ Do you want a teacher who already has a coven you can join? Are you willing to start a coven with a new teacher? What type of social learning environment will you thrive in?

❖ Are you willing to attempt long distance training? If so, will you need to meet periodically in person? Will you travel, or will your teacher travel, or would you take turns traveling to each other? If you study with a long distance teacher, will you also want or need a local group to practice with? If you already have a local group, how will training with a long distance teacher affect your group?

❖ Is the person you're considering as a teacher as qualified as they claim? Are they being authentic with you from the start? Ask them how they learned what they know, and ask if they can provide references, either from other students or from their own teacher. If they are self-taught and haven't had any other students, ask to see them in action before you decide if you think they're qualified to teach what they do.

❖ How will you compensate your teacher? Traditional Wicca has strict taboos against charging money for Craft training, but that works because Wicca's initiatory structure allows its training to operate with a "pay it forward" system. A teacher does not expect their students to pay them back for their education, but they do expect them to pay it forward to their future students. In a sense, students become indebted to their tradition, not their teachers, as they gain their education, and they pay off that debt by teaching the tradition to others. This makes traditional Wiccan teachers extremely hesitant to take on a student unless they are reasonably confident that the person will stick with the tradition and eventually pass it on. If you choose to work within an existing initiatory training structure, chances are that structure will already include guidelines for what the student must offer in return. In Spectrum Gate Mysteries we decided to stick with the idea that initiates pay their debt to the tradition rather than to the teacher, but we expanded our definition of that payment to include any service they offer our community, not just teaching. Not everyone wants to or should be a teacher, and there are many other ways to contribute to a coven and to the Craft. We expect our students to support our community through their continued participation, but we don't limit what that participation needs to look like.

Guiding Students

In an ideal world, the only people training students are qualified teachers, and every student gets the education they need. Unfortunately, the real world does not often conform to our ideals. Teachers can be hard to find, and all too often those seekers who are competent enough to organize a group also end up training it. The complexities of Pagan pedagogy are well beyond the scope of this book, but if you end up in charge of a group of people looking to you for education, consider the following:

❖ What does the student want to learn, and what are you qualified to teach? Be honest about what you know, and about what you don't know. If someone wants to learn something you haven't really learned yourself yet, that's OK—you can learn it together as training partners or a study group. You don't have to pretend to be knowledgeable or skilled in something you aren't really familiar with. It is infinitely better to be forthright about your own abilities and competencies rather than trying to look impressive for a student or a group. This way you don't just teach content; you also teach honesty.

❖ Screen potential students for compatibility with your teaching style. What are their expectations of the student-teacher relationship? Do they match your own? Are they willing to put in the level of effort you want from your students, and are you willing to put out the level of effort they want from their teacher? What are the student's strongest learning styles, and can you teach to those aptitudes?

❖ How do you want your teaching to be structured? Casual meetings? Formal lessons? How often do you want to meet with your student, and how many and what types of assignments will you give? Will your teaching include elevation rituals? If so, does your student want elevations, or are they unsure? Are you willing to begin teaching a student while they gather information and decide whether or not your elevations are right for them?

❖ Would you be creating a new coven with this student? If so, is the student willing to start one with you? If you are already part of a coven, would your student need to join it? How does the rest of the group feel about that?

❖ Are you willing to teach long-distance? Can you manage long-distance teaching without periodically meeting face to face, or will you need to plan regular visits? Will you travel to the student, or will they travel to you? Does the student have a local group to practice with, or local training partners?

❖ What is your goal for the student? Do you want them eventually to become a long-term member of your working coven? Do you want to teach them your style of Coven Craft so that they can someday start their own group and pass it on to someone else? Do you just want to help them get their own coven started and then leave them to their own devices? Often students won't know right at the outset how they want their full training to culminate, so it can help to establish short term goals, and reevaluate next steps as you accomplish each one.

Ranks and Elevations

Elevations are rites of passage that can both motivate a student and document their progress. This is, however, a secondary function of these rituals. The true purpose of elevations is to guide the seeker on a journey through themselves, to explore and deepen their relationship with the divine, and to give them a unique and inarticulable sense of self, purpose, and spirit. Part of what makes elevation rituals effective is not knowing exactly what they will be like when you go into them. They are Mysteries, and would be spoiled by preconception or expectation.

Consequently, I will not be sharing scripts or descriptions of the Spectrum Gate Mysteries elevation rituals. I will, however, present the general purpose of each elevation, describe each of our ranks, and list the curriculum offered at each one. Remember that there are many magical and spiritual systems out there with different types of elevations and ranks. Our way is not the only way, just one of many.

I must also note that a teacher is absolutely required in order to navigate our elevations. Obviously if you don't know what the ritual is, you need someone else to officiate it for you, but a teacher is necessary for the entire process of the elevation journey, not just for the rituals themselves. Each rank comes with its own unique challenges, and teachers customize those experiences for each individual seeker.

Accepting a Student

A student is someone who has reached a formal agreement to begin the Spectrum Gate curriculum with a qualified Teacher. We do not commemorate this agreement with a special ritual, as students often begin their training uncertain of how deeply they want to commit to the Craft. If the student wishes, we will make an announcement in circle to the rest of the group that someone has begun their training, but otherwise we give them space to explore the fundamentals of our craft without any external pressures.

Sometimes a person will become a student and join a coven at the same time. We most certainly do favor coven joining rituals, but these should be highly customized celebrations that are unique to your group.

Consider what makes you—all of you together—who you are, and think about how you would welcome a new member into that community.

Suggested Student Curriculum:

- ❖ Grounding, Centering, and Shielding
- ❖ Pagan Etiquette
- ❖ Basic Self-Reflection

Dedication

A dedicant is someone who has committed themselves to studying the Spectrum Gate Mysteries ritual system, developing their personal spirituality, and exploring their connection to divinity. The dedication ritual involves a commitment to each of these. The rank of dedicant is named for the dedication a person feels to their own spiritual path—it is a state of learning and being, and of letting your spirituality flourish as an integral part of your identity.

Dedicant is the first official rank in our system, and it is a stable one. Certain other ranks are transitional, meaning someone is eventually expected to pass through them to something else. A dedicant, on the other hand, can stay a dedicant forever if that's what they choose. Depending on their arrangement with their teacher and their coven, they might be expected to complete all dedicant curriculum, but after that they could remain a dedicant for as long as they like if they are content with their practice as is, or if they do not feel called to any other ranks.

Suggested Dedicant Curriculum:

- ❖ Basic Energy Work
- ❖ Elemental Associations
- ❖ Altar Setup
- ❖ Basic Circle Casting
- ❖ The Wheel of the Year
- ❖ Lunar Associations
- ❖ Paths of Power
- ❖ Understanding Possession
- ❖ Negotiation

❖ Introduction to Mythology

Neophyte

A Neophyte is someone actively pursuing Spectrum Gate Mysteries initiation. When a dedicant decides they want to pursue further training, they request initiation, not "neophyte", as neophyte is a transitional rank. The neophyte ritual thrusts the student into a state of intense introspection and reflection, often fraught with confusion and turmoil, in which they must seek their spiritual calling. Usually this ends with the student declaring their Call of Service and becoming an initiate. On rare occasions the student discovers that initiation is not right for them at all. They too must leave the liminal space of neophyte, but they can choose to go back to being a dedicant.

Suggested Neophyte Curriculum:

❖ Discernment
❖ Craft History
❖ Officiator's Roles
❖ Regalia
❖ Ritual Tools
❖ Ritual Hosting
❖ Supporting the Possessed
❖ Ethics
❖ The Call of Need
❖ Intermediate Self-Reflection
❖ The Call of Service

Initiation

When a neophyte has explored themselves spiritually and discovered the sacred Work they must do, they are ready for initiation. The initiation ritual recognizes the spiritual transformation they have undergone, and welcomes the self they have become into the Craft. Initiate is another stable rank; an initiate can stay an initiate forever, and the initiate curriculum is aimed at developing proficiency with the Spectrum Gate Mysteries ritual system.

Suggested Initiate Curriculum

- ❖ Elemental Spirits
- ❖ Advanced Energy Work
- ❖ Advanced Circle Casting
- ❖ Self-Care

Wandering

Wanderer is another transitional rank, and denotes someone actively training to become a traveler. Like neophyte, the wandering ritual pushes the student to reevaluate themselves and their spiritual path. Travelers are meant to be pillars of support for the community, so a wanderer must learn to support themselves well enough to also support others.

At the same time, a wanderer searches for their own way of contributing to their community, and must choose one of three paths to becoming a traveler: the path of the leader, the teacher, or the adept. Leaders feel called to work with organizing and motivating people. They study various social and political models, and prepare to run their own Spectrum Gate Mysteries coven. Teachers feel called to educate. They study teaching techniques, examine their strongest and weakest teaching styles, and prepare to train new students. Adepts feel called to serve their community, but through neither teaching nor leading. They discover and develop their own way of contributing to their coven, and to the Craft.

Becoming a wanderer is a commitment to moving forward. Once begun, there is no way back, but all ways ahead are open. A student wanders until they learn how to travel.

Suggested Wanderer Curriculum:

- ❖ Essential Ritual Design
- ❖ Ritual Tool Design
- ❖ Advanced Self-Reflection

One of the following:

- ❖ The Path of the Leader
- ❖ The Path of the Teacher
- ❖ The Path of the Adept

Traveling

A Traveler has completed the Spectrum Gate Mysteries training system, and is able to continue their personal journey with the knowledge and skills they have developed. Our sacred paths never end, so our elevations are not aimed at attaining an ultimate degree or a fancy title. Our goal is to reach a state where we can continue our journey on our own, forging our own path, learning from everything around us, and positively contributing to our spiritual communities as we go. Traveler is a stable rank, but that does not mean we never change, never learn, never modify our practice. As wanderers we search for the journey that calls us. As travelers we journey with purpose.

Final Thoughts

So you're already doing this, or something very near to it? Great! We know we're not the only ones, but not enough of us are talking about it, and too many people think they're alone. There are seekers out there trying to find a place that values their experiences just as much as anyone else's, and we're trying to show them that they have options. We don't claim to be the only option, or even the original option, but we're here, and we're willing to help.

Our way is not the only way. Our group likes these concepts, but other groups or individuals might not. That's OK. If you don't like our approach to circle casting, or our take on the Sabbats, or one of our rites of passage, feel free to do something different.

This book covers a lot of information, but there is still much that it doesn't cover. I purposely refrained from writing certain things here, because some things must be learned from a teacher, and many things must be learned by doing. Much of the Craft means nothing if you merely read it. One must practice our art in order to truly understand it. There is also much more to be said on topics like magic, Sabbats, rites of passage, and education, but a comprehensive discussion of these subjects was simply beyond the scope of this book. Perhaps future volumes will address those matters in greater depth, but for now I offer merely an introduction and overview.

If you are already initiated in a Craft tradition, think about what I've written here, and compare it to what you learned. Those dots that look like they connect? They do! Pull those pieces together and make a cohesive system that works. We do not want to be the only coven practicing Spectrum Gate Mysteries, and we don't want our way of going about it to be the only way. Add your own experience and insight, and show us how many hues we can shine in.

Appendix: Energy Work Exercises

Grounding, Centering, and Shielding

The term "grounding" can refer to both getting rid of excess energy and to connecting with one's physical surroundings. High energy states can overwhelm our senses, making it hard for us to feel connected to what's around us. The connection we create when we ground not only stabilizes us like the tail of a kite, but also gives us a channel through which to vent excess energy, allowing us to maintain a level awareness of both spiritual and physical inputs.

"Centering" means to become present in and aware of your physical body. It can also involve aligning your energy body with your physical body. When we center ourselves, we become aware of where we end and other things begin, yet maintain our connection to the world around us.

When we shield, we create a buffer zone between ourselves and every-thing else. It can be firm and reflective when we need protection, or soft and permeable when we want to connect. A shield is an energetic manifes-tation of our personal boundaries.

The following meditation will guide you through basic grounding, centering, and shielding. Before you begin, consider the following:

❖ What energy source do you feel most comfortable connecting to? Most Pagans start out grounding into the Earth, as Earth energy is naturally stable and helps people feel solidly connected. Every-one is different, though, and some have better success grounding into the air, or into a body of water like the ocean or a river. It's best to start with a natural energy source rather than grounding into something man-made, as human energies are just as unpre-dictable as human beings.

❖ What does your energy body look like, and how will you want to align it with your physical body? The two don't need to be per-fectly matched, but in order to center properly, there will need to be some type of harmony between the two. If your energy body and your physical body are vastly different shapes, try looking for a midpoint in each, and then center those midpoints. You might feel some dysphoria at first, but accepting your energetic and physical bodies as different yet equally important parts of you can become tremendously affirming. Even if you yearn to change your physical body in some way, acknowledge and accept the difference just in that moment. Your future form can be whatever you wish, but in that instant be what you are at present. You will know you are successful when you feel a sense of spiritual presence within your own flesh. This can be harder than it sounds, so don't worry if it comes slowly, or if that sense of presence isn't immediately strong. The more you practice, the easier it gets.

❖ How permeable do you want your shield to be? Consider starting with something gentle, leaving plenty of energetic flow through your buffer. Rigid shields can feel suffocating and isolating, especially for highly energy sensitive people who aren't used to them. It's best to start soft, and gradually solidify your protection until it feels just right. Pick a metaphor that suits you, like a screen door keeping out the bugs, or the feeling of a soft sweater that keeps you just warm enough without making you sweat.

If you can remember the following meditation and guide yourself through the steps from memory, wonderful. If not, consider having someone read it to you, or record it and play it back for yourself. Reading and meditation occur with very different brain waves, so you're unlikely to be successful trying to do both at once. You might also consider adding specific descriptions and metaphors to this meditation that help you. If you tend to visualize energy, add a description of what you want your shield to look like. If being centered comes with a certain scent, add that cue to the meditation. If certain music helps you meditate, play that as well. Use whatever tools work best for you.

Find a place to rest comfortably. Sit or lie down, close your eyes, and relax. Take a moment to simply feel your body. Are you warm or cold? How does the air smell? What can you hear aside from these words?

Feel your proximity to the energy source you chose, your ground. Reach out to your source and connect with it. Feel the energy of your source flow into you, recharging your personal reserves, and feel any excess energy flow out to your ground, leaving you contentedly balanced. Bask in that sustaining connection.

Now keep that connection, but gently direct your awareness back to your body. You are still part of the world around you, but feel where it ends and you begin. Let your energetic body and your physical body align, two harmonious parts of a balanced spiritual entity.

With your awareness fully integrated at your center, create an area of personal space around you. Feel this space as yours, and create a permeable boundary at its edge. Allow yourself to feel through it, but only just enough, and just what you need.

You are here. You are yourself. You are your own.

Passing Oranges

"Passing Oranges" is part game, part practice, part magical working. It likely has other names in other groups, but I call it "Passing Oranges" because that's what we used the first time I ever played it—oranges. Really, you can do this with any object, but it can be fun to use something edible.

Choose an item that you can pass around your circle. As each member takes it, they receive energy from the person who handed it to them, add some of their own energy to it, and then pass all that energy on to the next person. The object becomes a physical vessel for the energy, allowing people who aren't yet sure what to look for a tangible cue for where the energy is.

As the item travels around the circle multiple times, pay attention to how it feels. Does it get warmer? Heavier? Do people feel different while they're holding it? Can you sense where it is even when it's not in your hands?

Once you get comfortable passing energy in a general sense, try using a particular type of energy. Start off with something that's easy for everyone in your group to focus on. For example, if your group has a special affinity for the elements, use elemental energy, or if your group is particularly visual, use colors.

When you're reasonably confident with your ability to pour a specific type of energy into your object, you could try using a type of energy that everyone would want to bring into themselves. For example, perhaps you could all use a little extra luck, or maybe the energy of kinship would help your members bond with one another. If your object is something edible (like an orange), you can focus the desired energy into that food, and then share it with each other when you're done as a small magical feast. Just make sure you share the food with everyone. I once saw someone eat the entire orange by himself, and he was high for hours afterward!

Dropping the Ball

"Dropping the Ball" is a simple partner exercise that develops both energy sense and energy manipulation. One person waits with their eyes closed and one hand held out flat. This tends to work best with the person's non-dominant hand, but try both anyway and see which works best for you. The other person holds both hands together as if shaping a ball of snow or clay. This person slowly fills their hands with energy until they have created an energy ball about the size of a large orange. When they feel that their energy ball is complete, they drop it onto the open hand of their partner. When the partner feels the energy of the ball on their hand, they open their eyes.

About The Author

Thista Minai is a Priestess of Artemis, polytheist, spiritworker, ordeal facilitator, Third Degree High Priestess in the Blue Star Tradition of Wicca, Tashrisketlin Master Ritualist, and founder of Spectrum Gate Mysteries. She has more than fifteen years of experience with designing and conducting rituals, performing various types of energy work, and has taught lectures and workshops on a variety of topics including modern Paganism, sacred sexuality, ordeal, and kink. Thista applies the knowledge gained from her master's degree in education to developing better curriculum and support structures for students of modern Paganism and spirituality.

Printed in Great Britain
by Amazon

73636347R00109